Braveheart Woman

Rising Above: The Incredible Faith in Perseverance and Forgiveness.

Jocelyn C. Hughes

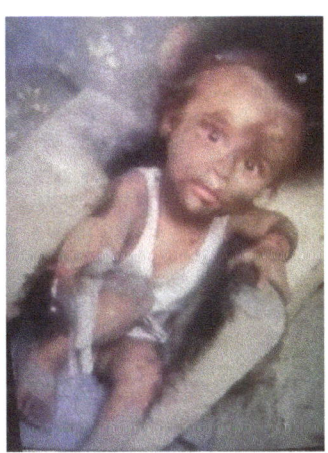

Copyright © 2024 Jocelyn C. Hughes

All rights reserved. No part of this publication may be reproduced, distributed or transmitted in any form or by any means, including photo– copying, recording, or other electronic or mechanical methods without the prior written permission of the publisher, except in the case of brief quotations embodied in critical reviews and certain other noncommercial uses permitted by copyright law.

All Scripture quotations, unless otherwise indicated, are taken from the Holy Bible, New International Version®, NIV®. Copyright ©1973, 1978, 1984, 2011 by Biblica, Inc.™ Used by permission of Zondervan. All rights reserved worldwide. www.zondervan.com. The "NIV" and "New International Version" are trademarks registered in the United States Patent and Trademark Office by Biblica, Inc.™

Contents

Dedication 1

Introduction 3

Chapter 1 God Cares for a Five-Year-Old Girl 5

Chapter 2 Tied to a Coconut Tree 12

Chapter 3 Never Give Up 17

Chapter 4 Faith and Belief 21

Chapter 5 Be Courageous and Positive 24

Chapter 6 Courage and Determination 29

Chapter 7 Never Give Up and the Power of Imagination ... 36

Chapter 8 Persistence and Faith 43

Chapter 9 Imagination and Determination 51

Chapter 10 Sleeping Under the Bridge 56

Chapter 11 A Miracle Newborn Baby on the Street 61

Chapter 12 A Real Runaway Bride 67

Chapter 13 Cruel Husband, Choking to Death 75

Chapter 14 By Faith, the Rainbow Dream Becomes a Reality 80

Chapter 15 My Comatose Son 85

Chapter 16 Answered Prayers 89

Chapter 17 Confusion and Hospital Gowns 95

Chapter 18 Hot Chocolate and Court in Los Angeles 100

Chapter 19 A Baby Born on the Freeway 112

Chapter 20 Miracle Patient 118

Chapter 21 The Building and Rainbows 131

Chapter 22 Single Motorcycle and Bank Miracle 135

Chapter 23 Forgiveness Is the Best Revenge 144

Chapter 24 Angel Miracle 150

Chapter 25 Impossible to Possible 160

Chapter 26 A Surprise Gift from God 165

Chapter 27 Miracles from an Angel on a Motorcycle and Tsunami Yolanda 170

Chapter 28 Surprise Trip to Australia 182

Chapter 29 Rebuilding the Past 191

Chapter 30 Knockdown Never Knockout 195

Conclusion 202

About the Author 205

Disclaimer

The information in this book is intended as guidance based on personal experience only and should not substitute medical care. Always consult your doctor first before beginning a new regimen.

Dedication

This book is dedicated to my family and to my grandparents, Mr. and Mrs. Escolastico Cueva Sr., and to my mom, Onofra Cueva Carator.

I especially dedicate this book to my sons. My four boys, James, Joel, Abraham and Joshua gave me the courage to keep going on my journey. They inspired me and are loving kids. I'm so proud of all of them, my jewels of sons.

I would also like to dedicate this book to all my teachers in elementary and high school.

To children, battered women, single parents, rape victims, the elderly, and anyone who has experienced neglect, abuse, malnourishment, or suffered from a lack of love from their family - have faith, believe in yourself, and never give up.

Escastico Cueva Sr.
My grandfather, 105

My 4 sons Joel, Abraham, James Joshua

Introduction

My story is one of deprivation as a child, perseverance as a young person, and becoming a successful mother and businesswoman. I share some of my narratives in this book to help others overcome negative situations, give hope, and be motivated to never give up, no matter life's circumstances. In *Braveheart Woman*, only those happenings that I felt strong enough to share are included, as I am still healing from many of the offenses I have experienced in my life. As you read, you will understand what I experienced and how I survived.

I was neglected, nearly abused to death many times, and the victim of malnutrition. I was rejected by my family, lacking their love. With great dedication, care, and intent to make sure I would achieve my dreams, I pursued my education. I encountered many noes and turned them into yeses.

I turned my life experiences into a business, and they are shared in the book. My sense of curiosity led me to research healthy foods, and because I was concerned for others' health, Angelcare Miracle Mix products were the result of my studies. These healthcare food supplements have multiple benefits to help the body function optimally.

The presence of God in my life since childhood is the one single factor that has sustained me. To this end, my life has been an incredible journey. Now, I want to share my journey with you in

Braveheart Woman: A Journey of Perseverance, Faith, and Forgiveness.

My life story illustrates the strength of my mind and the genuine presence of the Lord Jesus Christ in my life. From a childhood of neglect, abuse, and hunger, I have emerged as a successful inventor, businesswoman, and proud mother of four sons.

This book intends to share my journey with you, the reader. We can learn from each other's experiences to be strong, and I hope you will learn from my past and know that you, too, can persevere and be resilient.

Chapter 1
God Cares for a Five-Year-Old Girl

My name is Jocelyn "Joy" C. Hughes. I was born on June 20, 1968, on one of the most beautiful paradise islands in the Philippines: Bantayan Island, Cebu. Cebu is one of three central provinces in the Philippines, a country that is comprised of 7,641000 islands.

My mom and dad weren't married, so when she became pregnant with me, she didn't want me. When I was only a few months old, my mom gave me to my father, who raised me in my early years. I was abandoned as I never lived with my mother or siblings. In 1972, when I was four years old, my dad passed away, so my maternal grandparents took good care of me at that point. I was the only grandchild who lived in their house, along with my aunt (my mom's sister). My grandparents loved me, and I loved them like my mother and father.

When I arrived at my grandparents' house, my grandma would read the Bible to me. Every morning at 3:00 a.m., she would wake me up and read the stories in the Bible for three hours. I would listen to her read, and she would explain the stories to me. It was the first book I learned to read at the age of 4 ½ years old. The Bible taught me how to be positive in life even though I was without parents who could have guided me at a young age.

I was five years old when my aunt began assigning me heavy tasks and chores to do in the house, such as cleaning the whole house, including my grandparents' and aunt's bedrooms, the kitchen, and the dining area. I was also tasked with filling jars with water from the well every day; it was our only source of water. I was allowed to eat my lunch or dinner once I finished my job. My aunt would always hit my leg with a stick or belt or whatever she could hold in her hands. At the time, I didn't totally understand why she hit me, but as I got older, I realized that she didn't like my dad or the fact that my skin color was darker than the rest of the family.

One day, I was handed all the containers and clay jars for water and went to the well. I needed to fill them up, including the bucket for the bathroom. Imagine a very tiny and skinny five-year-old little girl having to do all the chores in the house because she was forced by her aunt. My stomach was always empty because I could not eat until I finished all the household assignments. I felt so lonely and was constantly crying. I tried to please her, but I was rejected. I felt like I was not part of the family, but I always reminded myself that my grandparents loved me.

When I was six years old, I asked my grandpa, "Take me to school." I wanted to study, I wanted to learn how to write and read, and I wanted to wear a school uniform like other pupils. He agreed to take me to school.

On my first day in school as a grade-one pupil, I had nothing to bring; no bag, no school supplies, not even a pair of shoes because no one could buy them for me. My grandpa didn't have money to do so. It was not uncommon for me to go to school or church without slippers and wearing the clothes that my grandma made for me. The only clothes I owned were three dresses made from flour sacks and three pairs of underwear. I was careful to wash the clothes by hand, as I didn't want anything to happen to what little I owned.

When the class started, my teacher asked me, "Where is your bag? Do you have a pencil? Paper?

I said, "Teacher, I don't have those. I'm sorry."

My teacher told me, "Tomorrow, bring your pencil, notebook, and paper."

"Yes, ma'am," I replied.

After school, I walked back to my house. I went to my room and changed my clothes, then went to the kitchen to see if there was any food to eat. Luckily, I found pieces of banana cooked in boiling water. I ate it and drank a glass of water; then, I went to the well with the empty containers and jars to fill them with water.

I was so sad because I didn't have anything to bring to school the next day like the teacher requested. But I went back on the second day of school anyway. My teacher asked me, "You did not bring your pencil and paper again? I told you to bring it."

I cried and said, "Teacher, I don't have any of those things, but I want to learn. Can you teach me, please? I promise I will be a good student. I just want to learn how to write and how to read. Please! Don't make me go home."

I didn't want to go home. I wanted to stay and learn. Determined to get an education, I wasn't leaving the school, so my teacher told me to sit down; she didn't have a choice! She didn't like that I came to school without any supplies. Suddenly, the girl beside me, my seatmate, gave me one sheet of paper, and she went outside and cut her pencil in half. She gave me half, and I thought, *Oh! How lucky I am!*

She smiled at me. She was so lovely to me when she said, "It's okay."

Then my teacher yelled at me, "I will give you another chance tomorrow to bring your own school supplies!"

And I replied, "Yes, ma'am."

When I went home, I prayed to God, asking for His help. I didn't have any school supplies. I tried to ask my schoolmate, who also happened to be my second cousin, and other family members for the items, but no one bought any supplies for me. With the exception of my grandparents, all my relatives told me that I should not go to school. Later in the afternoon, I walked to my neighbors' house, which was some distance from my grandpa's house, to help them harvest the vegetables in their garden. They gave me some of the food after working so I could take them home. My neighbors were pleased! They said I made their job so easy because I helped them.

I brought the vegetables home, and I told my grandmother not to cook them so I could take them to school the next day and give them to my teacher and the other teachers. There were six teachers in the school, including the principal. I wanted to provide them with the vegetables in exchange for a sheet of paper and a pencil and so they would let me stay in school to study and learn.

I didn't have any plastic bags to put the vegetables in; however, I was thinking of something I could create. I saw some banana trees in our backyard, just a few meters walk from our house. I grabbed the dried banana leaves from their branches, and I created some string by pulling the leaves into strips. With the banana leaf strings, I made six bags. "Yeeey!" I shouted because I was so happy. Then, I divided the vegetables between the bags and put them inside a giant empty sack of rice.

On the third day, I went to the school early, and I brought the six bags of vegetables.

When all the teachers and the principal arrived, they noticed that I had come so early, and they saw me having a hard time carrying the sack of rice, which had six bags of vegetables inside it. The teachers started laughing! They asked me why I was bringing the sack with vegetables to school.

"Sir, please don't make me go home! I want to study!" I begged and cried in front of them. "I have vegetables; I can give all of you one bag each. I want to study, please!" They were all silent. "Can you exchange my vegetables for a pencil and paper?" I asked. "I will bring vegetables every day. Please, help me, sir."

As the principal looked at me, I couldn't help the tears from falling down my face. I cried until he said, "Okay!"

Suddenly, my tears were gone, and they were replaced with a smile. I was so happy to stay in school. The next day, the principal asked me to come to his office. He offered me a job cleaning the classroom's toilets and helping the teachers with various tasks. Sometimes I was assigned to work in the canteen as a sales lady, selling snacks and food during lunchtime or break time.

I started working in the school when I was six years old, and then I would go home and do all the chores in the house, like cleaning and filling all the containers with water. Even though I was now going to school, if I didn't finish all my household chores, I couldn't eat.

My aunt hated me for some reason. All I knew was that she always hurt and punished me. She even gave me food that was spoiled or had mold on it, so sometimes I would skip eating. My cousins and other relatives lived on the other side of my grandpa's house, which was really about a city block in the distance from his. They didn't like me and called me a monkey because of my dark skin and curly hair.

Mr .Tinga my elementary teacher

My Elementary teacher Mrs Villaceran

Chapter 2
Tied to a Coconut Tree

When I was seven-and-a-half years old, I almost died because of a beating I received from my aunt. She lost a large amount of money that was in her wallet. She didn't lose it; it was stolen, and I knew who had done it. It was my cousin next door, but I never told my aunt about it because I knew she wouldn't believe me. She loved all my cousins. They were her favorite, and she gave them food and bought shoes for them. So, my aunt accused me!

She believed I stole her money because she saw me with money in my hands, even though she didn't know where the money came from. It came from my job at the school, where I sold snacks. The money I earned, I saved. My aunt dragged me to the coconut tree in the backyard, and she tied my hands behind the tree. I was kneeling down, and the ants were biting me. My aunt began spanking me with a stick from a guava tree. A guava tree is made of hardwood, so every time I was struck, it cut the skin on my body. I didn't know how hard I was being hit until I saw blood from the wounds on my legs. It flowed so fast; I didn't know what to do.

All I could do was cry because my hands were tied up. After being beaten for a long time, I couldn't feel the physical pain anymore; my body was numb. I was tied up from 8:00 a.m. until 4:30 p.m. the day, and for most of the day, my aunt abused me. I was accused of stealing her money. After hours of repeated strikes,

I didn't have any more tears. It progressed to the point where I asked my aunt to just kill me; I didn't want to suffer this hell any longer.

All my cousins watched and laughed as my aunt continued to abuse me. They were the ones who stole the money, yet they never helped me. My mom happened to be passing by the house at the time, and she didn't try to rescue me. I was hungry and thirsty, as I was given no food or water. I begged my aunt to give me some water. Instead, she held my chin up so my head was tilted back, covered my mouth with one hand, and, with her other hand, poured the soda into my nose. She may have been trying to drown me, but instead, the soda flowed from my nose, down my throat, and into my mouth, so I tasted it. But still, my mouth said, "It is not enough."

While I was tied to the tree, I prayed to the Lord and prayed Bible verses that I learned from reading the bible. I asked myself why I was born in this world to live like I am in hell. Was I born to be punished and constantly abused? As the day progressed, I didn't feel the pain anymore, but I prayed Psalm 23 because I wanted to die rather than suffer at the hands of my aunt.

At 4:30 p.m., my grandpa came home from work. When he arrived home, he rescued me right away. He cried when he saw me tied to the coconut tree, almost dead and downhearted. He untied my hands, picked me up, and carried me into the house. I was almost dead due to the blood loss from the open wounds on my legs. I had been accused of something I never did.

My grandpa took me to the only hospital on Bantayan Island on his tricycle, which was about a one-hour ride. He peddled as fast as he could after working a long day. When we arrived at the hospital, the doctors stitched and closed all the wounds. To this day, I still have the scars to remind me of that horrible beating.

My grandpa was so mad at his daughter, my aunt. He was so angry that he went looking for her when we returned home, asking, "Where is she?" My aunt had left the house and ran to Cebu to hide from him. My grandpa chased her, but since she headed to Cebu, he didn't pursue her, as it is a large city, and he needed to figure out where to start looking for her. Upon returning home, still angry, he grabbed his stingray fishtail and went to my cousin's house. He shouted to my cousins, "Who among you here has the money? Answer me!" He continued furiously, "If you don't tell me right now who stole the money, then I will punish all of you."

Suddenly, one of my cousins confessed! He said he divided the money among his siblings, and some of them had spent it already. My grandpa was so upset with them that he wanted to put them all in jail, along with my aunt. The parents of my cousins begged my grandpa, "Don't put them in jail. Do not report them to the police." Reporting the theft to the police would be a big issue and bring shame to their family.

From that point forward, I was terrified to stay in my grandpa's house; I was traumatized because of the extensive abuse that I had suffered from my aunt for the past few years. The coconut tree incident is only one of many stories that I could share. I wanted to get out of that house, but I had no choice, as I wanted to finish my elementary studies. Rarely did I sleep in the house. Instead, I chose to sleep in the barn with the goats or with the chickens in their coop. When I was about eight years old, my grandpa made a tree house for me, so I had my own hideout to avoid being harassed by my aunt.

Eventually, my aunt returned to the house. Since the day she tied me to the coconut tree, I was scared to go home as I didn't want to see her. A few weeks later, I attended a bible study instead of going home after school. This was not my routine, so when I didn't show up after school, my grandpa was worried. When I arrived home from the Bible study, I saw my grandpa on the terrace of the treehouse he built for me. He was so happy when he saw me because he thought I had run away. He hugged me and asked, "Why did you leave?"

I replied, "I am not leaving you, Grandpa. I was just attending Bible study." I cried to him about everything that had happened. I asked him why I was born into this world. I said to him, "If this is my life, then I wish my mother had aborted me when I was in her tummy." I even asked God to take me from the world; I couldn't bear it at all. I questioned God about why He created me to be part of this world. If I was only going to live with pain, then there was no point in living at all.

But I realized I was wrong to question Him. I shouldn't have because He is truly unique. I always read the Bible, especially when I was feeling nervous about my aunt. I started to memorize texts in the Bible that comforted me and gave me strength so I could keep going and stop questioning God.

The trauma I experienced at my grandpa's house did not hinder me from pursuing my studies or reading the Bible. It made me courageous. The Bible was my parents, my guidance, and my hope. I memorized Psalm 23, Psalm 121, Proverbs 3:5, Psalm 91, and Hebrews 11. I learned them and repeated them continuously.

Chapter 3
Never Give Up

Reading the Bible suddenly gave me strength and hope to keep going. With the help of my grandparents, who always loved me, supported me, and always taught me to never give up and to always believe in miracles, I began to feel better.

My grandpa shared with me a story about a mango tree. He said to me, "Look at this, Joy! This mango plant is still small, but one day, it will grow and become a tree that has many branches, green leaves, and plenty of fruit. But before that can happen, this mango tree will have to surpass many trials. The storms, heavy rains, floods, strong winds, and heat from the sun. People don't mind this mango plant because it is small for now, but when the tree is enormous, and it bears flowers and fruit, then people will notice—especially when it has a lot of fruit.

"In short, humans do not care about the life of a tree, if it will survive or die. But, by the time the mango tree grows and is abundant with fruit, humans will take the step to own it. That is why you should be like a mango tree. One day, people will recognize your capability and your ability. Have faith in God, keep going, and never give up, my daughter.

"One day, when you grow up, you will be successful, and you have to share your fruits with others. Those people and your relatives who hate you, you must replace them with love so God will bless you more." When my grandfather told me this, I cried. But in my mind, I now knew that God had something for me. The Lord knows I am strong like a mango tree, and I know that God created me for a purpose.

My grandfather gave me the courage not to give up, but I was always afraid of my aunt. I only felt secure if my grandpa was at home. Sometimes, I stayed in the barn with many chickens and goats, as I didn't want to be in my grandpa's house if my aunt and I were by ourselves. My grandma could not help me because she had a mild stroke, and I was so nervous whenever I saw my aunt's face. There were times I would hide inside the kitchen cabinets or under my grandma's skirt. On one occasion, my aunt was looking for me, and my grandma was sitting in the backyard while I was hiding underneath her skirt. My grandma never told my aunt where I was hiding.

My childhood could have been better. I never had toys like dolls. I didn't even have playmates; all I did was do chores in the house and work at school. I never had love from my parents or relatives other than my grandparents. Only my grandparents loved and cared for me. I was still lucky, though!

My grandma always sang me the song "What a Friend We Have in Jesus,"

written by Joseph Medlicott Scriven (1855). She sang it to me until I memorized it. The message of this song inspired me.

"What a Friend We Have in Jesus"

What a friend we have in Jesus,
all our sins and griefs to bear!
What a privilege to carry
Everything to God in prayer!
O what peace we often forfeit,
O, what needless pain we bear,
all because we do not carry
Everything to God in prayer!
Have we trials and temptations?
Is there trouble anywhere?
We should never be discouraged;
Take it to the Lord in prayer!
Can we find a friend so faithful?
Who will all our sorrows share?
Jesus knows our every weakness;
Take it to the Lord in prayer!
Are we weak and heavy-laden?
Cumbered with a load of care?
Precious Savior, still our refuge—
Take it to the Lord in prayer!
Do thy friends despise, forsake thee?
Take it to the Lord in prayer!
In his arms, he'll take and shield thee;
Thou wilt find a solace there.

This song provided me comfort and strength to keep me persevering throughout my life.

Chapter 4
Faith and Belief

In 1975, when I was seven years old, I slept in between my grandparents because I didn't want to experience my aunt's wrath. One night, I dreamt that I was passing big buildings with their lights on, and the sunrise was shining on them. In the background, behind one of the buildings, was a rainbow with the colors of the sunrise, which reflected the light in the morning. The next scene of the dream was in the evening when I would again pass the same buildings, with the light of the sunset reflecting on them. The background was a beautiful rainbow reflecting the same colors as in the morning. In the dream, I passed the building multiple times, and it made me so happy. Then I woke up. I began dreaming the same dream many times, two to three times a week.

The dream repeated itself for many years while I attended elementary school. One day, I told my grandfather about the dream, and he said one day I would live in that place. But this was the only thing he said. He needed to tell me what country or where these buildings were located.

Finally! It was my elementary graduation day. I was so happy. In my mind, I knew I would finally be able to leave the island where I lived with my grandparents. I couldn't wait for that day. I approached my teacher, and I asked her to give me my diploma because it didn't matter if I would be able to attend the graduation ceremony or not. I needed to go.

She exclaimed, "No! You should be there."

I explained to her, "But I don't have anything to wear. I have no dress and no shoes for my graduation."

My teacher bought a pair of shoes and a dress for me so I could attend the graduation ceremony. All the teachers and the principal pinned the ribbons (school awards) onto my dress instead of my family because none of my relatives attended, even though they were invited. Even my grandpa was in the city on graduation day, but he didn't attend either because he had to work; he was a cook and was preparing for a party that day. During the ceremony, the teachers handed me my medals in recognition of being an honor student.

I was crying, not because my relatives didn't attend my graduation, but because I graduated from sixth grade with honors. All my hard work and determination paid off, and I had now graduated from elementary school in Balintawak, Bantayan Island, Cebu.

After graduation, I planned to go to Cebu City, to look for a job. I asked my grandpa about it, and I explained that I wanted to study at the high school. He granted me permission to pursue my desire. I went to the city looking for a summer job that I hoped would last for two months before the opening of another school year. I was delighted that while I was on Bantayan Island, I had a friend in church and a business owner permitted me to ride on a cargo ship from the island to Cebu City (another island), Cebu, Philippines.

It was hard for me to look for a job, as I was only eleven years old. I knew it was likely that no one would accept me, but with my faith and determination, I was able to find a job and study at the same time. The elder of the church I attended in Bantayan Island owned a store in the city, so I was able to get a job helping in their store. While I attended elementary school, I worked for the same church elder and his family, so the elder knew of my home life and needed to sustain myself. Along with my studies, I helped clean their house and cared for their kids. I received no help from any of my relatives. I had nothing, but I had a Father in heaven who is the Father of the Fatherless.

Chapter 5
Be Courageous and Positive

I taught myself how to be positive. This mindset will help you become someone who is not afraid to face fears and can stand up to adversity and take action when needed. The Bible taught me to be strong and not give up on my prayers, even though I was praying and asking God to die so I didn't have to suffer anymore. God had other plans for me. He gave me the courage to persevere. Courage, like everything else, has to do with who you are; it starts in your mind and has its roots in your past, and my past was full of neglect and abuse.

With a positive mindset, my fears began to dissolve, and I was ready for whatever the day would bring. You can choose to be positive or negative, believe it or not. Either way, you can get the life that flows from that decision. If you think your world is hostile, then it will be that way. Believe it will be positive, and it will be positive. Stay inspired! You are the engine of your dreams.

After my graduation, I had faith and believed that I could continue my journey to study in high school. I looked for a job to sustain myself and continued my studies. I was very motivated despite my unfavorable circumstances.

The Bible was my number one guide through every challenge of every day. Below are two scriptures about having faith from many in the Bible. Hebrews 11:1 tells us,

"Now faith is the assurance of things hoped for, the conviction of things not seen" (ESV).

And Ephesians 2:8 states,

For it is by grace you have been saved through faith, and this is not from yourselves, it is the gift of God - (NIV)

Faith is the opposite of doubt. I believed God's word as it is written in the Bible, and I still do. I think when the Word of God says in Mark 11:24,

Therefore, I say to you, whatever things you ask when you pray, believe that you receive them, and you will have them.

So, I continued to pray. Let me share a story about my grandfather's friend who was sick and having faith. The man was very ill and needed medical attention, so Grandpa and I walked with him to the hospital. We walked three hours with him because we couldn't afford to pay for a taxi or a jeep ride, and we wanted to be sure he arrived safely at the hospital. As we walked, I listened to their conversation. My grandpa gave the following advice to his best friend, "Have faith in God and believe in Him. You will be healed; you will be better."

"Yes, I will." His friend replied.

When we arrived at the doctor's office, which was located inside the only hospital on Bantayan Island, the doctor checked my grandpa's friend's chest and blood pressure. He gave the elderly man a prescription for his ailment. I'm not sure what caused him to be sick, but the doctor told him to take the medicine three times a day for seven days. After a week, we returned to the doctor's office for a follow-up appointment and to check on my grandpa's best friend's improvement. We walked to the doctor's office again, but this time, his friend was so happy and already felt better.

My grandfather asked his friend, "Where did you buy the medicine?"

His friend said, "I never bought any medicine. The doctor advised me to take the medication three times a day for seven days. So, I boiled water, added the prescription paper, and cooked it until the paper melted. Then I drank it three times a day for seven days. That is the only thing I took. You told me that, didn't you?"

We started laughing because the friend's actions of boiling the paper in water were accidentally practical. We all knew it was the man's faith that healed him. I kept listening to their conversation. We were still laughing as we walked to the office. I laughed so loud and for so long that I peed in my underwear. My grandfather laughed so loud that he peed his pants, too.

I was laughing in front of the doctor. I couldn't stop myself. The doctor said to my grandpa's friend, "Okay, you feel better now! Did you take the prescription?"

Grandpa's friend said, "No! You never told me to buy it. You told me to drink it three times a day for one week. And my best friend told me to have faith and believe I would be healed."

Then the doctor laughed. We all laughed.

I would like to share some affirmations with you from Ray Davis's article called "28 Belief Affirmations and Original Quotes."

- "I am ready, willing, and able to take my life to the next level! Today I DO!"
- "The fire ignited by one moment of belief can burn down a forest of doubts."
- "Every event, every relationship, every circumstance in my life is working for my benefit."
- "WHATEVER I need ALWAYS comes my way."
- "It's not the mountain I conquer, but myself. I'm reaching for the top of the mountain, and my day in the Sun is here."
- "Today, my whisper becomes a shout! I CAN! I CAN! AND I AM!"
- "Today, I am sharing my talents with a world thirsty for what I have to offer!"
- "You can choose to believe or not believe. Either way, you get the life that flows from that decision."[1]

Bible Verses About Faith

James 2:17 ESV

"So also, faith by itself, if it does not have works, is dead."

Hebrews 11:6 ESV

"And without faith, it is impossible to please him…"

---

[1] Ray Davis, "28 Belief Affirmations and Original Quotes," The Affirmation Spot Blog, November 2, 2011, https://affirmationspot.me/2011/11/02/belief-affirmations-and-original-quotes.

Romans 10:17 ESV

"So, faith comes from hearing, and hearing through the word of Christ."

Chapter 6
Courage and Determination

I focused on my dream, the dream about the city with the buildings. It inspired me; it made me not want to give up. I was going to live there someday. I knew it! Now, it was 1981. I was eleven years old and looking for a summer job. The summer would be another journey for me. I was a child who was full of disappointment. It felt like I was alone in this world, homeless. I wished my dad was still alive, and I hoped he was by my side. Even though he had died years ago, I knew he was with me; I could feel his presence.

It took me thirty-six hours to travel from Bantayan Island to Cebu City, I spent 24 hours waiting at the pier and another 12 hours traveling on the boat to my destination. I was traveling alone and needed help finding a job. There was no food to eat on the boat, and I only brought two cooked bananas and one bottle of water with me. I packed two sets of clothes and my Bible in an empty rice sack and had one hundred pesos in my pocket ($5). The money was given to me by my teacher and the principal during my graduation. When I was on the boat, I knew God was with me wherever I went and would go.

The words in the Bible that gave me courage were from Psalm 68:5, which tells us God is the Father of the fatherless and abandoned children. I survived without eating food and just drank water for several days. I had walked to the pier barefoot, so after buying a pair of slippers for my feet, I had no money left, either. By reading my Bible, I knew that Matthew 4:4 assured me, "Man shall not live by bread alone, but by every word that comes from the mouth of God" (ESV).

Finally, I arrived in Cebu, and I began looking for a job right away. Even housekeeping would be OK as long as it could sustain my stay and my food. I searched until I found a friend who I knew from church. She was so lovely to me; she let me work in her store. My job was to clean the whole store. But it would only be temporary because I needed to go to high school. No one would support me, but I thought I could work and study at the same time.

At eleven years old, I wanted to attend high school. Every school that I tried to participate in rejected me. They didn't accept me because I was underage, but I never gave up. I tried and tested. I kept asking people at the church I was attending where I could apply to be a working student. Sometimes, I was imagining that I was already in school, studying, and working at the same time. I had no idea where to go.

I asked my friend in the store if she knew someone who could guide me to which school that would allow me to work and study. She said, "I can! I can take you to the school. It is a private school, and maybe you can work and study there."

We went to the school. It was East Visayan Academy, which is a Seventh Day Adventist (SDA) school located in Bulacao, Cebu.

When I saw the school, I was so happy, and I imagined myself already there.

I knocked on the principal's office door. When he answered, I smiled and asked, "Sir, may I apply for a job and to study?"

The principal said, "Kid, you are too young to work. How old are you?"

"I am eleven years old," I replied.

He laughed! He said, "Go home, kid. You cannot work here, and besides, this is a private school, and it is expensive. Who will pay for your tuition?"

"I don't have anyone to help me," I explained. "I don't have family. My relatives have all rejected me. But I want to work so I can study."

"Where are you from?" The principal asked me. "What school?"

I said, "I came from an island, sir."

He finally told me, "We cannot accept you here. Look for another person to help you."

I went back to my friend's store for a short time, then in the afternoon I went back to the school again.

I knocked on the principal's door again, and when he answered, he looked outraged. "I told you to go home. You cannot afford to study here!"

"I have no choice," I explained. I went home again, but I still had hope that one day I could study there.

I continued to go back to the same school twice a day for two months. I kept knocking on his door. I was always smiling, hoping maybe he would accept me. One day, when he said, "I don't want to see you anymore!"

I was shattered, but I didn't want to give up. I was always crying because I was unable to attend the school. The day he told me that he didn't want to see me anymore was Friday, the last day of the week. Determined to attend high school, the following week, I returned to the same school. I said to myself, *maybe this would be the day*. I knocked again and smiled, with faith that God would answer my prayer.

The principal told me, "Finally, today is your last day, kid. By next week, the class will start, and I will not see you anymore." He laughed.

"I know, sir! But I am not going home until you accept me to work and study here." I said it with courage. I looked into his eyes and smiled. In my mind, the principal would say, *yes, I will accept you.*

But instead, the principal said, "Yes; however, I will give you an exam. You need to pass with ninety-five percent so you can work and study here."

He handed me the test paper, and when I saw it, I realized it looked very difficult.

"It is for fourth-year high school students," he said. "Geometry, Algebra and English are the subjects. You only have thirty minutes to take the exam, and it has one hundred questions. If you fail, you know what to do."

I was holding the test paper, and with my determination, I knew I could do it.

And I did.

In just twenty minutes, I finished the exam and gave it back to the principal. I smiled, and he was so surprised when he was checking it. I got a perfect score! I answered everything correctly.

When he saw this, he smiled at me, "How did you do it?"

I said, "God is with me. He helps me with the answers."

The principal didn't say anything. He couldn't say anything.

He gave me a job at the school in exchange for my tuition, as it was a private high school. For work, I needed to clean the boys' and girls' dormitories, cook for the students, and clean the office. This work just paid for my tuition, so I wouldn't be allowed to stay in the dormitory. In addition to my tuition, though, my food would also be accessible. I said, "Thank you, God, for answering my prayers, and I thank you, sir, for giving me a chance to study and work."

After this, I began looking for a place to stay, but no one would accept me, not even my relatives. I told the principal about this and asked, "Can I sleep in the cafeteria in the stock room?"

"Ok," he agreed, "but you will have no bed."

"It's okay," I assured him, and I slept in the stock room.

My two friends: Gina. Ababon, Guadalopi & ME

My high school teacher owned a store, and I worked for her on the weekends. Whenever I had free time, I would go door-to-door selling vegetables, fish, and anything I could find to sell outside the school's compound so I had money for my personal needs.

My relatives (mom, uncles, aunts, and cousins) who lived in Cebu City were surprised that I was in school. None of them would talk to me because they were ashamed of me. Some of my relatives were teachers at the school, but no one would help or talk to me. I was a working student, cleaning the school and cooking in the cafeteria. I would go to sleep late, and I wake up at 3:00 a.m. to start work. Then, at 8:00 a.m., I would go to class. I worked very hard for my uniform and pair of shoes. At one point, I had to put glue on my shoes because they broke, but I managed every day with the strength of our infinite God.

With my determination, faith, and belief, I did not give up.

Chapter 7
Never Give Up and the Power of Imagination

As I fought to be accepted into a school to study and work, my imagination was a powerful tool. When I knocked on the principal's office door, I imagined the principal accepting me already. While he continued to reject me, I visualized that I would be attending that school one day. My hardships pushed me to keep going. Positive thought patterns are conducive to creativity and imagination.

I attended East Visayan Academy from 1981 to 1985. From my first year to the fourth year, I worked as a student, and it was not easy. I pushed myself to survive, study, and work in the school, but sometimes I became discouraged. But my dream was to finish school so I could quickly get a better job. I persevered to keep going on my journey. I didn't have the life of an average child. I missed having a childhood and having fun as a kid. For friends and family, I was only a survivor who was still alive.

As a teenager, the only things I did to survive were work and study. Growing up was miserable because I was missing out on experiences that other kids my age were doing to have a happy life. I kept thinking, *why was I born only to do this? I don't understand.* I cried every day and night because so many things were missing in my life. But the Bible was my guide every day, and the Word of God comforted me every night.

I changed my thinking to a positive attitude so that I could persevere until I graduated. My classmates wouldn't even talk to me because they were rich and had money, and I was only a slave who cleaned the toilets and cooked, doing all sorts of jobs around the school. I had two best friends, and they supported and comforted me when I was crying about my hardships. So, I just kept myself busy and imagined that one day I was going to live wherever the buildings that I saw in the dream were located. I was still determining where the buildings were found, but that was where I dreamed of living.

One day, I went to the city library. I wanted to look for the buildings I had been seeing in my dream that continued while in high school. I looked through many books. In a history book about the USA, I eventually found the place I had seen in my dream. It was downtown Los Angeles, California. This was the place I would one day live.

I was three months away from graduating high school when there was a hurricane in Cebu. That day, there were torrential rains, and it was so windy. The storm was so strong that the roof of the cafeteria and stock room where I slept was ripped off by the wind. I was worried that I wouldn't have a place to sleep for only three more months before I finished my schooling. My principal told me I needed to look for a place to sleep because they would be fixing the roof and the cafeteria, so I did.

I asked a couple teachers, families who bought vegetables from me, and relatives, but no one accepted me to stay temporarily until school was over. I was disappointed. I went to the compounds that are located outside of the school building, looking for a place to stay because I didn't have money for rent. I couldn't afford it since I was still working and studying in school.

But I didn't give up; this was just another trial in my life. I said to myself, "I passed elementary school. That was hard, and I can do it again." As I kept walking outside the compound of the school, I found a small house made of bamboo with a very poor old lady sitting in the doorway. The house walls were made of Nepa (coconut leaves) and plastic only. The old lady had a daughter and a grandson living with her. The daughter was a single mom with a two-year-old son. The mom worked in a factory while the grandmother watched the baby. The old lady would always buy my wares every Sunday when I went door to door selling fruits, vegetables, and fish. I asked the old lady if I could sleep in her home for the last three months of my schooling, and she said yes. She explained that she had a mosquito net over her bed so we would be able to sleep together. I thanked her, and from that point on, I came home to her every night after completing my studies and chores for three months.

Sometimes, when the rain came inside the house at night, we would all move to one corner so we would not get wet from the rain. But I was happy to stay with this family because they accepted me as if I was part of their family.

On the day of my graduation, I was alone again. Nobody attended my graduation, even though I had plenty of cousins and relatives who lived near the school. I managed to buy my own clothes for my graduation from the second-hand clothes store.

After my graduation ceremony was over, I saw my relatives outside the church. They tried to congratulate me because they were all shocked that I graduated. None of my family helped me, not even with a single piece of paper or a notebook. They just ignored me and pretended I was not a relative. They were my uncles, aunts, cousins, and some who attended the same school where I studied at the same time. I was not happy to see them waiting for me. When I needed help, they didn't. But now they were outside waiting to congratulate me. Each one of them offered to give me a complimentary dinner for my graduation. I said, "No, thank you. I'm not going with you." I left and headed to the house of the old lady who had given me shelter.

When I got to the house, the family had prepared dinner and was waiting for me. I said, "I'm happy for your kindness." The old lady explained that she didn't have a gift for my graduation, but she cooked her only chicken just to give me something to eat. She made a soup with the chicken and vegetables. I was so shocked that I cried because I knew she only had one chicken, which gave her eggs for the baby. She had such a big heart, and I never imagined I would be so lucky to have someone outside of my family who loved me.

The old lady was another reason why I dared to keep going on with my life and not give up. God was using someone to help me and to love me even though I had been abandoned, rejected, and abused. God still loved me, and I refused to give up.

Napoleon Hill's book *Think and Grow Rich* tells us the following:

- Victory is always possible for the person who refuses to stop fighting. Only those who push through failure and refuse to accept defeat can truly understand how far one can go in life. The fact is the majority (of people) quit giving in when it gets complicated. The successful keep fighting. They find a way to win.
- It is literally true that you can succeed by helping others to achieve. Helping others is its own reward. The benefits you get from kindness and compassion towards others are far more valuable than any financial reward.
- Patience, persistence, and perspiration make an unbeatable combination for success.[2]

This book also says the following about persistence:

Persistence is simply the power of will. Willpower and desire, when properly combined, make an irresistible pair. Persistence is to an individual what carbon is to steel. In uncounted thousands of cases, persistence has stood as the difference between success and failure. It is the lack of this quality, more than any other, that keeps

---

[2] Napoleon Hill, *Think and Grow Rich,* (New York: Beyond Words, 2011).

the majority (of people) from great accomplishment. As soon as the going gets tough, they fold.

If you're to accomplish the goal you set for yourself, you must form the habit of persistence. Things will get difficult. It will seem as though there is no longer any reason to continue. Everything in you will tell you to give up, to quit trying. It is right here that if you go that extra mile and keep going, the skies will clear, and you'll begin to see the first signs of the abundance that is to be yours because you had the courage to persist. With persistence will come success.[3]

Bible Verses about Never Giving Up

Psalm 26:2 NASB 1995

"Examine me, O LORD, and try me; Test my mind and my heart."

Psalm 38:9 NASB 1995

"Lord, all my desire is before You, And my sighing is not hidden from You."

1 Corinthians 9:24-27 NASB 1995

"Do you not know that those who run in a race all run, but only one receives the prize? Run in such a way that you may win. Everyone who competes in the game exercises self-control in all things. They then do it to receive a perishable wreath, but we can

---

[3] *Ibid.*

make it imperishable. Therefore, I run in such a way as not without aim; I box in such a way as not beating the air."

Philippians 4:13 NASB 1995

"I can do all things through Him who strengthens me."

2 Timothy 4:7 NASB 1995

"I have fought the good fight, I have finished the course, I have kept the faith."

Abondia Abillana 100 years old. She is the one who sheltered me for 3 months and cooked for me.

Chapter 8

Persistence and Faith

In the summer after my high school graduation in 1985, I joined the Philippines Publishing House, which is a Seventh-Day Adventist (SDA) organization that sells books door to door. It was a team of newly graduated high school students who sold the books to earn scholarships to attend college. I joined the group so I, too, could sell SDA books to make a scholarship to attend college and earn a business degree. Each team member had a goal, and if I reached mine, I could have two years of free college tuition. I was so excited to become part of the team and have this summer job because I wanted to go to college, but I didn't have the money, and I had no family to help me.

We were all students in the group; there were twenty-five of us. We would go door to door selling books. Our leader in the group directed us that we needed to work eight to ten hours a day, we needed to knock on every door to sell the books, and we had to sell books to pay for our food.

Every day, I walked miles and miles in my assigned area of Mactan, Cebu, City. In my neighborhood, there were significant buildings, and I was expected to knock on every door in every office building, as well as every house and apartment. I needed to walk because I didn't have the money to get a ride in a jeep or bus.

I would go out early in the morning so I could walk to the places I was assigned. I started knocking on every door, whether a house or office. If the person didn't buy anything, I had a free booklet to give to them. The booklet contained health information and Bible verses. I also carried with me books about health, children's books, and encyclopedias to sell. I kept knocking on every door, and I kept smiling, but people kept slamming the door in my face, telling me they didn't have any time for sales. After knocking on all the doors in my assigned area, I figured I had walked between five and ten miles every day. I would skip lunch because I didn't have money to buy food.

My leader gave me food each evening with the understanding that I would need to repay her when I sold the books. From the very first day of the first week selling door to door, I made no book or magazine sales. When I would arrive at the headquarters, and the other students were so happy because they received orders and sold books. I didn't say anything because I hadn't sold one book. I had only given away the free booklets.

During the second week, I experienced the same: I knocked on every door and didn't sell any books or get any orders. I was kneeling and praying to God to give me sales, but nothing. My knees began to scab from kneeling and praying three times a day. The third week passed, and again, no sales. I went to my assigned neighborhoods, and I attended every house and office. I knocked and knocked, but I would need someone to buy even one book from me.

I asked the Lord when I prayed why no one liked me enough to buy books from me.

Yet, I didn't give up. I kept going, and I kept smiling at every person I met them, but I decided they didn't like me. After all, they didn't buy any books because the people would slam the door in my face or didn't talk to me. I practiced how to sell the books. We had training, and I memorized the how-to approach. I thought, *why doesn't God give me sales? I want to go to college.* I was so excited to start the job, but I was having no luck.

Every time I went home, my leader said, "There is something wrong with you. You are withholding something."

I said to her, "No, I keep smiling at people. Some don't even open the door, some open the door, then slam it, and some talk to me but never buy."

My leader instructed, "Change your approach."

So, I changed my approach but still needed to sell books. One day, she accompanied me the entire day, but no one bought any books. By this time, one month had passed without a single sale. Some students had already reached their goals because their relatives had bought the books from them, so they went home.

But me? Not one sale. I was so discouraged with myself and asked why, but the next day, I needed to go out again. And again, a whole day and nothing. Six weeks passed. Then, seven weeks passed. I still needed sales. Finally, it was the eighth and last week.

After this final week, we needed to go home, whether I sold any books or not.

My last day at work was a Friday. I told my leader that I didn't want to go out today. I wanted to stay and clean the house. My dream to go to college was useless because I needed more money to go. I had yet to sell one book. I had only given away thousands of free booklets during the two months I worked for the publishing company.

The leader told me that we were only working a half-day, and we were to return to the living quarters by 1:00 p.m. since it was our last day to work. Since it was the previous day to sell books and everyone would be returning home on Sunday, I followed her command. But I went with no bag, no flyers, no samples, and no books to give away. In my mind, I wanted to give up. All I wanted to do was get out of the house and return at 1:00 p.m. as instructed.

When I left the house, I cried to the Lord and said, "Why doesn't anyone want to buy from me? I have been suffering in this world since I was a child, with no parents and no family to care for me." I was crying as I walked on the dusty road, and I reminded myself of a scripture in the The Bible states, "Call to Me, and I will answer you and show you great and mighty things, which you do not know" (Jer. 33:3 NKJV).

So, on Friday, the last day of selling books, I said out loud, "Lord, help me. This is my last day. I want to go to college, but I cannot do it." Then I remembered what my grandfather said to me:

trust in the Lord all the time. No matter what, I will be faithful, honest, and trustworthy, so wherever I go, people will love me. And my grandmother told me never to give up. Even if the storm is knocking you down, even if the sun is too hot, you need to keep standing and keep going. Don't quit, and in the end, miracles can happen. I remembered the dream from my youth about living in the USA. My imagination and my desire to live in the United States kept me going.

As I walked, I decided that the first home I encountered, I would stop and stay there until 1:00 p.m., when it was time to return to the house. I walked about a mile, and the first house I saw had an old man sitting on the balcony. The man was an American who was visiting his son and grandson in the Philippines.

I smiled and asked, "Can I sit down?"

He said, "Yes," and asked, "Where did you come from?"

"I'm a student working a summer job selling books for a scholarship, but I need to reach a goal. After eight weeks of trying to sell books, I don't have any sales. I don't have a family to help me, and I want to go to college, but I cannot because next week school starts."

The old man said, "Come inside the house and look."

I went inside, and his house was full of books. All the books that I was trying to sell what he already had on the bookshelves.

"Sir, is it okay if I wait here with you until it is time for me to go back to the headquarters at 1:00 p.m.?"

The old man said, "Okay, we can chat. I'm waiting to pick up my grandson from school. You can come to my house and look at the books I have in the library until I need to leave. We can walk together after lunch." So, I entered his house. The man gave me lunch to eat, which made me so happy because I was starving. We talked about the books he owned. I asked him if he had read them because some of them still had the plastic on them. After this, I read one of his books to pass the time before I had to go back to my headquarters.

When it was time, I said to the old man, "Thank you for giving me time to stay in your home, for listening to me, and for feeding me." I couldn't pay him back, but I offered to pray for the old man. After my prayer, he was ready to walk to pick up his grandson. The old man told me to wait for him outside so he could lock the house. When he came out the door, the old man handed me a check, and he said to me, "I have all the books, but I want to give you this check to buy the books so you can go to college. You can donate the books to the library." When I saw the amount of the check, it was precisely my goal to earn the scholarship for college tuition. He didn't know the amount of my goal because I had not told him; I just told him my life story. I was shocked because the check was from Bank of America. The check from Bank of America was very symbolic to me.

I said, "This is my dream country to live in. This is my dream." I kneeled before him and thanked him for his kindness, and I thanked

God for answering my prayers. We went our separate ways after lunch – he to pick up his grandson, and I returned to the headquarters with a check-in my hand.

I never gave up, and that was the reason I reached my goal to get my scholarship to attend college. My dream, imagination, and burning desire to move to the USA kept me going, and it kept me from giving up.

My prayers were answered because I didn't give up. The fruit I produced brings great joy to God, my Father in Heaven (John 15:8). God's power works best in my weakness (2 Cor. 12:9). Our sufferings produce perseverance, character, and hope, according to Romans 5:3-5:

"Not only so, but we also glory in our sufferings because we know that suffering produces perseverance; perseverance, character; and character, hope. And hope does not put us to shame because God's love has been poured out into our hearts through the Holy Spirit, who has been given to us".

Napoleon Hill's book says this,

If you give up before your goal has been reached, you are a "quitter." A QUITTER NEVER WINS, AND A WINNER NEVER QUITS. Write it on a piece of paper in letters an inch high, and place it where you will see it every night before you go to sleep and every morning before you go to work.[4]

---

[4] Napoleon Hill, *Think and Grow Rich,* (New York: Beyond Words, 2011).

Bible Verses about Persistence and Faith

Romans 1:10-12 NLT

"One of the things I always pray for is the opportunity, God willing, to come at last to see you. I long to visit you so I can bring you some spiritual gifts that will help you grow strong in the Lord. When we get together, I want to encourage you in your faith, but I also want to be encouraged by yours."

Matthew 7:7-8 NLT

"Keep on asking, and you will receive what you ask for. Keep on seeking, and you will find. Keep on knocking, and the door will be opened to you. For everyone who asks receives. Everyone who seeks finds. And to everyone who knocks, the door will be opened."

Me Joy Jocelyn Hughes

Chapter 9
Imagination and Determination

As much as I was discouraged, I also imagined and had the determination to attend college. After I received the two-year scholarship to Mountain View College in Mindanao, Philippines, from the only sale I had for the entire eight weeks. On the last day of selling books, it was time for a new journey. It was time to begin my new life in college. The book sale only covered my college tuition, so I needed to work for my food, dormitory, books, and personal needs. I still received no support from anyone.

Since I was late in registering for school and I needed a job to support myself, the only position available at the college was on the school farm, harvesting vegetables and tilling the soil. It was challenging work, what I would consider a man's job, but I took it because there was no other option, and I wanted a college education. I prepared the soil using two cows attached to a plow, which I maneuvered the best I could, as it was big and bulky. Sometimes, the cows ran too fast, and I wasn't strong enough to handle the plow and cows, so I would lose control and fall. I was fifteen years old at that time. I cried every night, but I was thinking about my dream of going to live in the USA. I kept believing that one day I would move there, so much so that I always wore the same t-shirt that had the words USA printed on it.

2 Timothy 4:17 is my favorite text in the Bible. I kept believing the promise of God. God stands at my side and gives me the strength I need for today. Metaphorically, I cleansed myself of the wood and clay in my life. I am better able to be used by God (2 Tim. 2:20-21) by reading the word of God.

Scriptures in the Bible that taught me determination include:

Do what is right and equip me for every good thing God wants me to do (2 Tim. 3:16-17).

God reveals His spiritual truth to me by His Spirit (1 Cor. 2:13).

Christ has set me free to experience true freedom (Gal. 5:1).

I'm learning to go boldly to God in prayer, and in Him, I find grace and mercy in times of need (Heb. 4:16).

God is my refuge, strength, and help in times of trouble (Ps. 46:1). When I get alone with Jesus, I find rest (Mark 6:21).

Because I believe in Jesus, I no longer live in the darkness (John 13:46).

I was created by God for His glory (Isa. 43:7).

God blesses me because I have a humble and contrite heart, and I tremble at his Word (Isa. 66:2).

As I acknowledge God in the morning, he makes my path straight during the day (Pro. 3:6).

I am complete in Christ (Col. 2:10).

I teach God's great truths to people who are able to pass them on to others (2 Tim. 2:2).

God is my stronghold in times of trouble (Ps. 9:9).

My hope is in the Lord (Ps. 40:7).

God's love for me is excellent! It reaches to the heavens (Ps. 58:10).

I am created in the image of God (Gen. 1:27).

Jesus came to the earth so that I might live an abundant life (John 10:10).

My glad heart gives me a happy face (Pro. 15:13)!

Jesus is the true Light that gives me light and life (John 1:9-10).

After my two years in college, I returned to Cebu City, Philippines, to get another job so I could continue and get a four-year degree. I was working in a factory as a sales manager, and the boss wanted me to continue my college education, so I studied Physical Therapy. She knew that physical therapy was a high-demand/high-paying job, and it happened that her husband also needed an excellent physical therapist. So, at her suggestion, I studied and graduated two years later with a four-year degree in Physical Therapy because I already had a two-year business degree. The college gave me an exemption, so what should have taken four years was accomplished in two. It was tough for me, but I managed to work because of the strength of God, who gave me more understanding. It was not easy, and I praise God for everything.

Quotes About Faith by Napoleon Hill

- "FAITH is a state of mind which may be induced by auto-suggestion."
- "FAITH is the head chemist of the mind. When FAITH is blended with the vibration of thought, the subconscious mind instantly picks up the vibration translates it into its spiritual equivalent, and transmits it to Infinite Intelligence, as in the case of prayer."
- "Have faith in yourself; Faith in the Infinite."
- "FAITH is the "eternal elixir" which gives life, power, and action to the impulse of thought!"
- "The foregoing sentence is worth reading a second time, and a third, and a fourth. It is worth reading aloud!"
- "FAITH is the starting point of all accumulation of riches!"
- "FAITH is the basis of all 'miracles,' and all mysteries which cannot be analyzed by the rules of science!"
- "FAITH is the only known antidote for FAILURE!"
- "FAITH is the element, the 'chemical' which, when mixed with prayer, gives one direct communication with Infinite Intelligence."
- "FAITH is the element which transforms the ordinary vibration of thought, created by the finite mind of man, into the spiritual equivalent."

- "FAITH is the only agency through which the cosmic force of Infinite Intelligence can be harnessed and used by man."[5]

---

[5] Napoleon Hill, *Think and Grow Rich,* (New York: Beyond Words, 2011).

Chapter 10
Sleeping Under the Bridge

In 1988, having just graduated from college, I went to Manila to begin the third part of my life's story. I started looking for job opportunities as a college graduate. I had completed two years of business and another two years of physical therapy and needed to take the mandatory national exam to be an official college graduate. I arrived in the capital of Manila, in the city of Manila, Philippines, with no money and not knowing where I could live.

I had one pocket filled with enough money for two weeks so I could take my exam and live inexpensively. After those two weeks, I didn't have a place to stay and had no food. I had relatives in Manila, but I didn't want to go to them because they had rejected me since I was young. They didn't care about me anyway; none of my family was close to me or would consider helping me.

After two weeks of looking for a job, I needed more money for food or a place to sleep. So, I decided to sleep under the bridge in Quiapo, Manila. I was seventeen years old at the time. I slept with cardboard boxes under me and then covered myself with more boxes to protect me from the elements. Once I was covered and ready to sleep, I would pray to God for the protection of my life. I had my Bible by my side, and my pillow was a small bag that was made from a sack of rice. I took a bath near the bridge by borrowing a bucket from the people who lived in a tiny cardboard house in close proximity to where I was sleeping. I just had to ask for water. I took my shower at 5:00 a.m. Because by 7:00 a.m., the running water by the bridge was turned off for the rest of the day.

I never gave up looking for a job. For a week, I survived with no food and only drinking water. Finally, I found my second cousin, who I had been searching for at the same time while I looked for a job. She had given me her address when she was visiting Bantayan Island while I was still in elementary school and told me that if I ever saw or moved to Manila, I should contact her.

She sold slippers near the pier where the big cargo ships were loading their cargo in Quiapo, Manila. I told her I had just graduated from college and was looking for a job. She asked me where I lived, and I explained to her that I was sleeping under the bridge in Quiapo without a blanket. I told her that I was using cardboard to cover my body, and it was also hiding me under the bridge. I was not afraid because I knew God had sent angels to watch over me. I had my Bible, and I kept reading it all the time because it was my protection.

My second cousin felt sorry for me, so she offered me a job helping her at the store selling slippers, so I would have money to buy food. Unfortunately, she could not offer a place to live because her boyfriend paid the rent where she lived, and he wouldn't allow anyone in their apartment. Even though I couldn't stay with her, sometimes she would walk with me to the Quiapo bridge because she was worried about my safety. I continued to believe God was watching me, and I never gave up. Every time I was sad, I would thank God because sadness turned into joy in my life. I would remember how God had saved me since I was a girl, and I knew He was always with me.

A month had passed, and I was still sleeping under the bridge. My second-degree cousin married her boyfriend and took her to Saudi Arabia. She left all her slippers to me, so I sold them to earn money. Like my cousin, I sold the slippers in the street near the harbor where the big ships would dock.

One day, a general of the Philippine Army saw me as I was selling the slippers and asked me where I was raised. I replied from Cebu. The general felt pity for me and told me that he would buy all my slippers and would give me a job at the Army hospital. When he said we should go to where I live so he could buy all the slippers I to sell, I explained that I was sleeping under a bridge in Quiapo. He was worried because I was a young woman sleeping in an open area. When he offered me the physical therapy job in the hospital, I was happy because God was watching over me and sent someone to help, and I knew it.

Many texts in the Bible encouraged me and are proof of God's protection. I didn't worry about everyday life because God knows my needs and meets them, and I make His Kingdom my primary concern (Matt. 6:25-33). Jesus shows Himself to me because I love Him (John 14:21). I know that because Jesus died for my sins, I am no longer separated from God. I live in close union with Him (Rom. 5:10).

The fruit I produce brings great joy to God, my Father in Heaven (John 15:8). God's power works best in my weakness (2 Cor. 12:9). Through the energy of Christ working powerfully in me, I teach others His truths (Col. 1:29). I have been saved, not by works, but grace, so that I might do good works (Eph. 2:9-10). My faith makes me whole in spirit, soul, and body (Mark 5:34). When I call out to God, He answers me. He tells me things I would not know otherwise (Jer. 33:3). Because I place my hope in the Lord, my strength is renewed (Isa. 40:31).

As I follow Jesus…as I walk with Him, I have peace (Luke 24:36). Because I obey Jesus, I remain in His love (John 15:10). The cross of Christ is my power (1 Cor. 1:17). My God meets all my needs (Phil. 4:19). God is my refuge and strength… always ready to help me in times of trouble (Ps. 46:1). God gives me strength when I am weary and increases my power when I am weak (Isa. 40:29). Because I place my hope in God, I can soar like an eagle, run, and not grow weary, walk and not be faint (Isa. 40:31).

The following are some of my favorite affirmations written by Dr. Lorretta Stanley and I would like to share them with you here:

I AM Divinely protected and cared for by Angels.

God protects me every day, in every way.

I always chat with my guardian angels and receive special assistance whenever I ask for it.

I feel safe and secure, and I live my life openly.

I know I am safe, and God continually watches over me.

I have guardian angels with me every minute of the day.

When others are around me, they feel safe and protected.

I live in a protected and safe environment.

Being Divinely protected is a 'given.'

God is more steps ahead of me than I can even imagine.[6]

Susan Shumsky wrote the following in her book, *Instant Healing*, "I am in control. [I am one with God.] I am the only authority in my life. I am divinely protected by the light of my being. I close off my aura and body of light to the lower astral levels of my mind. I open my aura to the spiritual world and the realm of the divine. Thank you, God, and SO IT IS."[7]

"Like a flitting sparrow, like a flying swallow, so a curse without cause shall not alight" (Prov. 26:2 NKJV). I know God has always been by my side, and I know if my prayers are not answered, something better is ahead because I have faith and believe that God is watching over me.

---

[6] Loretta Standley, "Sample Protection Affirmations," www.DrStandley.com, accessed April 13, 2021,
https://www.drstandley.com/guidance_protection.shtml.
[7] Susan Shumsky, *Instant Healing* (New Page Books, 2013).

Chapter 11
A Miracle Newborn Baby on the Street

In 1989, I was eighteen when I began working in Manila at V. Luna Hospital (a Philippine Army hospital). One night, as I walked to the apartment of my brother and sister-in-law in Alabang Manila, Philippines, I heard a baby crying. I began looking to see where the crying was coming from, and I found the mother with her newborn baby lying on a cardboard box in the street behind the apartment complex. The mother was holding the newborn, with the umbilical cord still hanging from the baby.

I asked the mother what happened, and she explained that she was only fifteen years old. She had been raped by the wealthy boss of the house where she worked while his wife was abroad. She went to the hospital to have the baby. After the baby was delivered, they realized she had no money to pay for their services, so the next day, she was kicked out of the hospital. The young woman told me that she would not be able to return to her employer's home because his wife no longer accepted her. She was even afraid to talk to her parents in Bacolod because her employer also paid their salaries.

The baby was only one day old when she was removed from the hospital, and she had no place to sleep. She was lying in the streets with the tiny baby; she had no clothes for the baby. She was not able to produce any milk for the baby because she had not eaten or drunk anything since she was thrown out. After two days in the streets, no one had helped her. My heart melted with sympathy for the girl and her baby, so I wanted to help her. I asked my sister-in-law if she had milk for the baby and if the girl could possibly stay in her home, but the young girl was afraid of my sister-in-law and refused.

I was only renting a small room as I worked for the hospital as a physical therapist. I told my aunt, from whom I was renting a room in Munoz, Manila, about finding the fifteen-year-old girl in the streets who had delivered her baby three days before. My aunt asked how I could go to work if I cared for a baby. I explained to her I was going to help the mother and would make it work.

I gave them shelter, food, and milk for the baby. I also took them to the doctor. I wanted to help the mother feel better so she would be able to take care of herself and the baby. I told the young mother that I would help her for a month, then I would take her home to her own mother in the province so her family could help take care of the baby. The girl begged me to please not tell her mother; she didn't want her mom to know she had given birth.

After a month of helping the young woman and her baby, she told me, "I give you my daughter," and the girl left the baby with me. I was in shock. I didn't believe her, so I looked for the mother and hoped that she would return to my home, but she never did. One month passed, then two, and I realized the mother was not returning, so I went to the social service agency and told a social worker about the situation. She told me that the mother would return and I should keep the child. I was worried because I, too, was so young. I was only renting a room and had a new job, so I wasn't equipped to have a child. The baby was so tiny.

After two months, I registered the baby in my name. The social worker suggested I record the baby, as she was not written in the hospital when she was born. So, I used my last name on the registration because I didn't know the mother's last name. I found another girl to watch the baby while I was at work, and I would watch her every day when I came home from work. There were some nights I wouldn't be able to sleep because the baby would be crying or sick. Suddenly, I was a single mother, though I had no boyfriend or husband. It was funny because problems always find me! I don't look for them, but God knows that I will survive in any situation. Even my relatives thought it was crazy that I was a mother at such a young age, but I was happy to have the baby.

At the advice of the social worker and my aunt, I took the baby to my own mother in Cebu, the woman who gave me to my father to care for me when I was a few months old. I asked her and my sister, who lived together, to watch the little girl, and I would support her by buying milk and providing for the baby's needs. When my mother saw the baby, she refused to accept it because she thought I was lying to her. She thought I had gotten pregnant without a husband. I assured her that the baby was not my child, but I had encountered the baby and her fifteen-year-old mother in the street. After a month of sheltering the mother, she left the baby with me and never came back. Out of stubbornness, neither my mom nor my sister would help with the baby, so I took the boat back to Manila with the baby. My new plan was to find a babysitter for the baby.

I was nineteen now, and the baby was such a happy one-year-old girl. I was so happy because she started walking, and she would smile every time I came home from work. She brought me joy every day. I was working to support the baby and me, but, in the end, it was a blessing. Even though I was young and inexperienced as a mom, but I learned a lot about caring for others and grew as a person. God gave me the courage to help a child who was abandoned like me.

Before all the events of the runaway mom and my new daughter happened, I met an American boy who was studying the Tagalog language at the high school I attended in my final year. I was planning to go to the USA to visit him, but then my life changed, and I became a mom. I was starting to worry. How could I tell my boyfriend that I had a little girl with me? My uncle, the owner of the apartment, and my auntie, who was my mom's cousin, had seen the baby grow up from infancy to her first steps. She smiled all the time, and my aunt and uncle loved her as we lived with them.

They suggested that I give them the baby because I had no life. They encouraged me to go abroad with my boyfriend. I agreed with their suggestion, but I told them I was still legally the real mother of the baby. They told me they would adopt the baby from me and change her last name to theirs. I was never able to find the baby's real mother, so this was the best plan for the baby girl.

At the time, the President of the Philippines was Cory Aquino. So, when my auntie and uncle adopted my daughter at two years old, they changed her name to Cory Ybanez. She was thrilled growing up with my uncle and auntie. When she was 28 years old and married, she wrote me a letter when I first moved to the USA. It read:

Mom, I thank you for saving my life in the streets. You are my first mother, whom God sent me. I know I'm so thankful to God that He sent you to save my life. I was so excited to have you. My adopted mother told me.

Although another woman gave birth to the baby girl, I'm her mother. I will always be her mother, even though my relatives adopted her from me.

As I recall my life, I see God and His plans for me. I was struggling, but God was always there watching over me, and He used me to make a difference in other people's lives. I praise God for His love and mercy that gives me strength every day for my struggle and uses me to be a blessing to others. I'm so thankful to God who preserved my life. I felt like my life was on death row, but He always saved me, and my duty was to help someone like me who was an orphaned child, abused, and rejected. My goal in life is to make a difference around the world and to build orphanages in different countries for abused and neglected children so they can be helped and educated.

Jesus led me into Your heart that is full of wisdom. "Come and listen to my counsel. I'll share my heart with you and make you wise (Prov. 1:23 NLT). God, I pray to know Your heart more deeply. I desire love - so I will love others. "Do to others whatever you would like them to do to you. This is the essence of all thit is taught in the law and the prophets" (Matt. 7:12 NLT). God, I seek Your will with all my heart.

"So, if there is any encouragement in Christ, any comfort from love, any participation in the Spirit, any affection and sympathy, complete my joy by agreeing, having the same love, being in full accord and of one mind" (Phil. 2:1-2 ESV).

When I was growing up, my childhood was full of rejection and abuse. The Bible was and is my strength and my parent; I depended on the Word for my determination and encouragement.

Chapter 12
A Real Runaway Bride

After studying the Tagalog language, my American boyfriend returned to the USA. We kept in contact, and he was planning to return to visit me. As I waited for the young man, I worked in the Army hospital in Manila. I was nineteen years old. One of my physical therapy patients was a Filipino man who became *interested* in me. When he was feeling better, he was looking for a way to thank me for what I had done. He went to my mother and sister and told them that he wanted to marry me.

He asked them to arrange the marriage, and my family wanted me to marry him because they knew of my dreams of moving to the USA. I didn't know him very well or love him; plus, I had an American boyfriend already. My family arranged the marriage anyway, even though I didn't want to marry him. They planned the wedding and picked the date, but I refused to marry this man and didn't show up on the wedding day. A month later, my family was telling me that I needed to marry this man. I explained to my family again that I wasn't in love with him and I had a boyfriend in the USA and I was waiting for him. But my family didn't like my response, and they tried a second time to set up a wedding with the same Filipino man. Again, I didn't show up at the wedding ceremony because I didn't want to marry him.

My family was so mad at me for skipping out on the second wedding date. They were upset with me because they wanted me to marry this man so I could not go abroad to the USA with my American boyfriend. However, I was not happy with my relatives interfering with my life and did not want them dictating my life or the Filipino man who wanted to marry me.

They made a third attempt to set a wedding date with the man. This time, I went to the church, but I was so mad because my family continued to interfere. There were a lot of people sitting in the church, but again, I told my relatives that I wasn't going to marry the Filipino man. After this announcement, everyone who was invited to the wedding left the church and went home. I canceled the wedding again.

A month later, the man was talking to my family again and told them they must do something to convince me to marry him. They spoke to me, but I said, no, I was not going to marry him. The planned marriage drama continued, and my relatives arranged a fourth date for my marriage to the same man. The wedding day arrived. My godmother and godfather were both in attendance. All my clients and my co-workers from the hospital were at the church, as well as others. I was not happy but pretended to smile.

I didn't want to marry him this time either, but my mother collapsed in the church, and I thought she might have had a stroke or could have died. Since she collapsed, my family insisted that I agree to marry this man. So, I was a fool and listened to all of them;

I decided to marry him. I found out later that the man had paid my mom and sister money to marry him. I was sold to and married a man I didn't love.

After the wedding ceremony, my new husband and I were on our way to the reception. I wasn't happy, so I planned to run away once we arrived at the honeymoon destination, which was a two-hour drive from the reception. I explained that I didn't want to get married and had already run away from the wedding and man three times previously. When I told him the situation, the driver agreed to help me. I would give him money to help me skip the honeymoon. The plan was for me to leave between the reception and the honeymoon.

Following our reception, my groom, a couple of bridesmaids, and I got into the car. I had brought a piece of cake with me. While we were driving, I was making fun of the cake, and I was smashing the cake into my husband's face. As everyone was laughing, I asked the driver, "Can you stop the car? I'm going to go to the toilet."

As soon as I got out of the car, I began running away, and the driver started to drive without me and continued to the hotel where we were on our honeymoon that night. I went to the first house I saw and knocked on the door, still in my wedding dress and shoes. When they answered the door, I asked, "Can I borrow some clothes and change?"

They asked me, "Why are you running away?"

"Please," I said. "Let me get out of here before my husband finds me."

They gave me clothes to change into, and then they took me to the pier. I got on a boat headed to Mindanao from Manila. I had money hidden in my bra to help me travel. The only clothes I had were those that I was wearing.

My husband searched for me for two months. He spoke with my family, who said they believed I would be hiding in Mindanao because I had attended college there. My mom's cousins who lived in Mindanao sent someone to look for me throughout the city and in the churches. I was able to hide with a church member who was my grandmother's relative for two months. But one day, the Philippine Army entered the church and found me, and took me to Manila.

When I was back in Manila, that was when my life became miserable again. My husband started to abuse me right away. He took me to the bed so he could enjoy me and then started hitting, smacking, and slapping me because he wanted revenge for what I did to him by running away a couple of times from the wedding day and the honeymoon. I won't share the details, but he said he could do anything he wanted to me since I was his wife, and he did. I became pregnant right away, and he left me for those nine months, so I was stuck inside the army housing compound by myself. I was told that my husband was on assignment, but I didn't believe it. I think he left and had me watched by someone in the army so I could not leave my house. He even paid for army personnel to bring my food to the house.

When it was time to give birth to my first child, I went to my godmother's home to deliver the baby. I hadn't had any doctors' check-ups because I couldn't go out to see the doctor. It turns out that my baby was a twin boy, but only one survived. He died two hours after being born. I was so sad when I gave birth to them. My husband wasn't with me when I gave birth to them. My first son was born in March 1990.

My husband found out I gave birth to the baby. He returned, and this time, he tied me to the bed for his enjoyment, and after a month, I was pregnant again. He left me again. As an army wife, I was provided shelter, food, and transportation as needed, so I was cared for, but my husband was not in the home. He didn't return until I delivered my second son, who was born in September 1991.

When my husband returned after the birth of the second baby, he got me pregnant for a third time. I tried to fight him off of me because I didn't want to become pregnant again. He was strong, and I was weak, so my attempts to keep him off me were useless. He continued to abuse me when he was around me.

Even with the worst of times, God watched out for me. One of my clients was a judge in Manila, and when he saw the bruises on my arms, he asked me about them. When I explained to him about the abuse I was experiencing, the judge told me he would help me divorce my husband. I moved out of the house, and I gave birth to my baby alone again. But this time, it was my choice. I delivered my third son in March 1993 but was not happy. I now had three sons, was twenty-three years old, had no husband to support us, and I was miserable. My entire life was a whole of trials and tribulations. I was crying out to God, "Why have I been suffering since I was a child and while married? It is tough for me, and I'm going to give up." But God showed me I should not give up. I prayed to the Lord and asked, "Help me to get out of this mistake of my life. Why am I alive in this world?"

I started to look for a job where I could bring my sons to work with me. I did not want to return to my husband. I learned how to fight and not to give up all my life. I remember God saved me many times during my lifetime, especially when I was a child. I found a job as a physical therapist at a clinic. The doctor gave me patients in his clinic, and he allowed me to bring my three sons and put them in an extra room with the babysitter. I was forever grateful to the doctor, as I was able to continue working and support my kids.

Even though I was afraid my husband would look for me, I learned how to fight back with the help of my divorce attorney and say no to the abusive man so I could protect my kids. I would tell him that he was not allowed to come near me or my kids. I prayed to God, telling Him that I wanted out of this life and to run away from the Philippines. I didn't want to see my husband, so I would bring my boys with me to the clinic, hoping that he wouldn't come to where I worked. But that didn't stop him from going to my house, which was close to the clinic. He didn't care; so when he came to the house, he hit, slapped, or kicked me in front of the kids regularly.

I asked God to help me because my big dream was to live in the USA. I couldn't see it happening. My dream was drifting away, but I didn't give up. I said to myself, "I can do it," and continued imagining my dream.

> *"He who is not courageous enough to take risks will accomplish nothing in life."*
>
> *-Muhammad Ali*

I would like to share with you sixteen affirmations of courage:

- My fears are dissolving.
- I am ready for whatever today brings.
- I am not a worrier.
- I am bold and daring.
- Today, I take action.
- I am fearless.
- Challenges? They are my specialty!
- I can do this.
- I radiate great courage.
- I am ready for bold adventures.
- I possess the strength to deal with this.
- I draw on strength from God for this.
- I am filled with endless possibilities.
- I am a person of great inner strength.
- I've moved past doubt and fear.

- I am unstoppable.[8]

Bible Verses that Give Me Courage to Keep Going

Deuteronomy 31:6 NKJV

"Be strong and of good courage, do not fear nor be afraid of them; for the LORD your God, He *is* the One who goes with you. He will not leave you nor, forsake you."

Isaiah 41:10-13

"So do not fear, for I am with you; do not be dismayed, for I am your God. I will strengthen you and help you; I will uphold you with my righteous right hand. All who rage against you will surely be ashamed and disgraced; those who oppose you will be as nothing and perish. Though you search for your enemies, you will not find them. Those who wage war against you will be as nothing at all. For I am the LORD your God who takes hold of your right hand and says to you, do not fear; I will help you."

---

[8] Kathryn Drury Wagner, "16 Affirmations For Courage," Spirituality & Health, accessed April 13, 2021,
https://www.spiritualityhealth.com/articles/2016/06/20/16-affirmations-courage.

Chapter 13
Cruel Husband, Choking to Death

It was now 1994, and my sons were three years old, two years old, and nine months old. The judge who was helping with my divorce helped me get a job with his son, a doctor. In the Philippines, it takes a long time to have a marriage annulled, so while I waited for the paperwork to process, I was still technically married. The doctor allowed me to work while the boys would be in the other room with the babysitter. By now, my divorce is final, and my ex-husband lost his job with the army, thanks to the judge help. My ex-husband's mother told him where I worked, and one day, he showed up in hopes of wooing me back to him and to see the boys. I told him, "Don't come here anymore. I can support my kids and me and live alone. I don't want you to impregnate me and abuse me." He was so mad that I refused him judge'she grabbed my neck.

He began choking me and drowning me in the bucket of water in the bathroom. I was being strangled to death, and I heard my three sons and the babysitter crying. I was praying, *Lord, don't allow me to die because of my three sons; they are small.* My head was inside the bucket, and he was choking me. I saw the water and the light color rainbow. I opened my eyes to struggle and fight him, but I couldn't because one of his hands was holding me, and the other was choking my neck inside the water bucket.

I thought, *God save me,* and I moved my elbow and kicked his egg bowl. He dropped me, and I ran to the room where my boys were crying. I managed to lock the door to the room we were in, though he stayed in the clinic, waiting. A few minutes later, though, the doctor arrived. I was shaking horribly because of what had happened. I told the doctor about the incident, and he said my husband couldn't come to the clinic anymore. Nobody knew what happened, not even my family. I skipped death on that day because God saved me. God saved me many times in my life.

That night, I prayed to God and asked, "Why? This is too much to bear. I have had these trials since I was a child. They've tried to kill me many times. Why was I born like this? With no family or parents and a husband who abused me and tried to kill me many times? I cannot handle this marriage anymore! I want to get out of this country and leave my husband."

On that night, again, I dreamed of the dream I'd had when I was a child. The next day, I prayed, "I want to go to the USA, but how can I go? I have three small babies?" But I also said, "I won't give up no matter what? I have skipped death many times."

According to Justin Brierly in *Premier Christianity,* there are three main reasons why God allows us to suffer. One, "because God won't rob us of free will;" two, "because we live in a broken world;" and three, "because suffering can draw people to God." Though suffering can make people doubt God, it is a natural part of our world, and we must trust in God and his plans for us.[9]

"It is suffering that inspires these conclusions: fundamentally, they are desires that such a world should exist; in the same way, to imagine another, more valuable world is an expression of hatred for a world that makes one suffer: the resentments of metaphysicians against actuality is here creative."[10]

Bible Verses

2 Corinthians 1:3-4

"Praise be to the God and Father of our Lord Jesus Christ, the Father of compassion and the God of all comfort, who comforts us in all our troubles so that we can comfort those in any trouble with the comfort we from God."

1 Peter 5:10

"And the God of all grace, who called you to his eternal glory in Christ, after you have suffered a little while, will himself restore you and make you strong, firm, and steadfast."

Romans 5:3-4

"Not only so, but we also glory in our sufferings because we know that suffering produces perseverance, character; and character, hope."

---

[9] Justin Brierley, "3 Reasons Why God Allows Suffering," *Premier Christianity*, June 16, 2016, https://www.premierchristianity.com/home/3-reasons-why-god-allows-suffering/1704.article.
[10] Friedrich Nietzsche, *Will to Power*, (New York: Penguin Classics, 2017), 579.

Romans 8:18

"I consider that our present sufferings are not worth comparing with the glory that will be revealed in us."

Psalm 34:19

"The righteous person may have many troubles, but the Lord delivers him from them all."

2 Corinthians 4:17

"For our light and momentary troubles are achieving for us an eternal glory that far outweighs them all."

Romans 8:35

"Who shall separate us from the love of Christ? Shall trouble or hardship or persecution or famine or nakedness' or danger or sword?"

1 Peter 4:1

"Therefore, since Christ suffered in his body, arm yourselves also with the same attitude because whoever suffers in the body is done with sin."

1 Peter 3:14

"But even if you should suffer for what is right, you are blessed. 'Do not fear their threats; do not be frightened.'"

Galatians 6:2

"Carry each other's burdens, and in this way, you will fulfill the law of Christ."

Philippians 1:29

"For it has been granted to you on behalf of Christ not only to believe in him but also to suffer for him."

Isaiah 53:3

"He was despised and rejected by mankind, a man of suffering, and familiar with pain.

Like one from whom people hide their faces, he was despised, and we held him in low esteem."

Chapter 14
By Faith, the Rainbow Dream Becomes a Reality

I kept my dream of the buildings in Los Angeles, USA, in my mind every time I was crying or facing a hardship. I was struggling to grow up with no parents or family to support me, except my grandparents, but I only lived with them for six years. After my husband attacked me, I continued to pray to God for a way to leave my husband because of the abuse and a way to go to the USA. The very next week, God answered my prayers.

The judge who helped me with my divorce had traveled to Nevada in the United States. While he was there, his blood pressure rose, and he had a stroke. His wife asked me to get a visa and travel to Nevada to help with the man's physical therapy, as the American doctor would not release the judge to return to the Philippines until he had a clean bill of health.

I had been praying to God that I could get a visa and go to the USA; the USA, I saw it in my dreams as a child. Then God answered my prayer, and I was granted a multiple-entry visa. The judge's wife said, "Okay, you should go to the USA, and you can go back and forth between the USA and the Philippines to see your children." So, I said, "Yes," and in 1994, I went to the USA to help the judge for three months.

When I arrived at the Los Angeles airport, I needed to fly to Nevada, so I needed to sleep at a hotel near the airport. I walked out of the airport and called a taxi. I said to the taxi driver, "Can you take me to the nearest hotel because I'm going to fly tomorrow to Nevada?" The taxi driver sensed that it was my first time in the USA. I was young and asking questions about the city where I had just landed. Wanting me to pay a higher fare so he would make more money, the taxi driver drove me to downtown Los Angeles.

When I arrived in LA, it was the afternoon, and as the driver drove me through downtown Los Angeles, he passed many significant buildings. And when I saw the lights and one of the important buildings, I remembered the dream I had dreamt multiple times. I said to the driver, "Thank you for bringing me to this area." And I thanked God because now my dream had come true.

The taxi driver started laughing because he said he brought me downtown so I could pay a higher fare. I said, "This skyline is what I saw in my dream when I was a child. Now I'm going to live in this country. Thanks, God, for bringing me to this place." I saw the light and the rainbow behind the building. I said, "This is it. My dreams become reality."

I would like to share some affirmations I found in the article "Free Affirmations Dream Your Reality."

- "I dream my reality from my heart, and love abides in all."
- "I am dreaming my purpose into being right this moment."
- "Dreams are the foundations of everyday miracles."

- "I will dream a castle in my heart that holds the roots of my happiness."
- "I will dream the solution to today's challenge, and it will no longer be a problem, but a blessing."
- "Dreams show themselves to us in the bloom of a flower, the smile of a child and our own innocent in loving the rain."
- "In the brightest dreams, a shadow may appear. It isn't fear of failure. It is fear of getting our wish."[11]

"A goal is a dream with a deadline." -Napoleon Hill.

Bible Verses about Dreams and Visions

Ezekiel 11:24 NASB1995

"And the Spirit lifted me up and brought me in a vision by the Spirit of God to the exiles in Chaldea So the vision that I had seen left me."

Ezekiel 37:1 NASB1995

"The hand of the LORD was upon me, and He brought me out by the Spirit of the LORD and set me down in the middle of the valley; it was full of bones."

Daniel 2:28 NASB1995

---

[11] JmaC, "Free Affirmations Dream Your Reality," Bipolar Support Groups.com blog, April 2, 2014, https://bipolar4lifesupportblog.co/2014/04/02/free-affirmations-dream-your-reality/.

"However, there is a God in heaven who reveals mysteries, and He has made known to King Nebuchadnezzar what will take place in the latter days. This was your dream and the visions in your mind while on your bed."

Daniel 4:5 NASB1995

"I saw a dream, and it made me fearful, and these fantasies as I lay on my bed, and the visions in my mind kept alarming me."

Daniel 2:19 NASB1995

"Then the mystery was revealed to Daniel in a night vision. Then Daniel blessed the God of heaven."

Daniel 1:17

"To these four young men, God gave knowledge and understanding of all kinds of literature and learning. And Daniel could understand visions and dreams of all kinds."

Genesis 37:5-7

"Joseph had a dream, and when he told it to his brothers, they hated him all the more. He said to them, 'Listen to this dream I had: We were binding sheaves of grain out in the field when suddenly my sheaf rose and stood upright while your sheaves gathered around mine and bowed down to it.'"

1 John 4:1

"Dear friends, do not believe every spirit, but test the spirits to see whether they are from God because many false prophets have gone out into the world."

Job 33:14-15

"For God does speak—now one way, now another—though no one perceives it. In a dream, in a vision of the night, deep sleep falls on people as they slumber in their beds."

James 1:5

"If any of you lacks wisdom, you should ask God, who gives generously to all without finding fault, and it will be given to you."

Proverbs 29:18 KJV

"Where there is no vision, the people perish: but he that keeps Eth the law, happy is he."

Chapter 15

My Comatose Son

It was not easy to leave my three sons; they were only babies—four, three, and two years old. My kids were too small to come to the USA with me, so I left them in the Philippines. Going to a new country and starting a new chapter would be suitable for all of us. We would have a better life in the long run. It was hard, though; I cried every day for my kids as I was not there to take care of them. I was not happy, but for the future of my children, I did it. They didn't understand my situation because no one knew what was going on in my life. I kept it a secret; no one in my family knew either. I moved, as I thought it was best for my kids. I did not want them to suffer like I did in my childhood experiences.

I worked in a hospital at that time and sent money to my sister, my father's father, and my family to support my sons. I tried my best. After a year of living in the USA, I flew to the Philippines to visit my boys. Having listened to the advice of my family and pastor to give my husband another chance and forgive him, I was ready to bring him and my sons to the USA. My husband would take care of the kids while I worked. I would be the sole supporter of the family. So, I changed my plans and was willing to give my husband a chance. But it was not God's will for them to return with me; my husband didn't want to go to the USA, so I decided not to bring my kids with me. Chapter 17 provides more details.

I left my boys with my sister and husband, and they continued to attend the Seventh Day Adventist (SDA) school until they were older. I sent money to their father and my sister to support them. Once again, I left my boys and returned to the USA by myself. It would have been too hard to care for my sons since I would have been a single, working mother of three young kids. To add to the situation, I learned that I was pregnant when I went for my physical exam before flying back to Los Angeles. There were more problems ahead, as now I would have four children.

One day, I got a call from one of the school's teachers telling me that all three of my kids were in the hospital, and one had collapsed and was unconscious. She told me she also noticed a lot of bruises on the bodies of my kids. My kids were small, and I was so worried. It turns out my husband and sister were using the money I sent to support the kids for something else. The kids had no food to eat and suffered from malnutrition. Unfortunately, every time I called to talk to my boys, they could not tell me what was happening because my husband and sister had manipulated them into not saying anything to me. My kids were abused by my sister and their father. Not one family member told me about the abuse because they were scared of my husband and sister.

I was so sad when the teacher called me. I said, "Can you take a picture and report this to the police? My kids are suffering abuse from my sister and their father." I worried every day about my sons. I needed to fly to the Philippines immediately because of the emergency. I talked to my immigration lawyer, as I wanted to get kids right then. My lawyer told me that the boys had green cards. Everything was ready; all I needed to do was purchase the airline tickets and fly to the Philippines to pick them up. But I was not able to go right away.

When I arrived at the hospital, all my boys were sick. My two younger sons were in a different hospital. The boys all suffered from malnutrition and had lots of bruises. They had collapsed in school, and the teacher brought them to the hospital. My oldest son, who was eleven years old, was comatose. I was in shock at what happened to my three boys because of the cruelty of my sister and husband. They wanted money, not to take care of my boys.

If my kids tried to tell me what happened to the money, they would be abused. Their father would hit them with a belt, and my sister hit my oldest son in the head with a chair; that is, my oldest boy became comatose. I learned that my oldest son would hug his younger brothers while they were being beaten to protect them—they all have scars, but he had the most. I was so mad at my family for the suffering they had caused my kids. I could not have imagined my life like this. Why are my kids suffering? My oldest son was in a coma; I cried to God.

I told the hospital no one was allowed to visit my kids in the hospital. I wanted to protect them because of the cruelty of their father and my family. After two weeks, I had to return to the USA because my youngest son, Joshua, had been left with his teacher in

Los Angeles. My kids were still in the hospital, though. I cried to the Lord, "Why would you allow that to happen to me and my kids? My frustration is high." But I didn't give up.

Day and night, I kneeled to God and asked Him, "Please give me strength to face this problem again." I spent a lot of money paying the hospital bills. I had so many loans because I was flying back and forth to the Philippines almost every week to see my kids, especially my oldest son. It felt like the burden was too much to carry; my problems were non-stop. But I did not lose hope; I kept holding onto the promise of God to show me miracles again.

Because God had saved me so many times as a child, I said, "Lord, I know You are there. Please help me; my problems are too much to bear." My two younger sons were out of the hospital after three weeks, but my oldest son was still in a coma. I would not give up. I still believed my son would wake up. I knew God was faithful to His promises.

Chapter 16
Answered Prayers

While my oldest son was still in a coma, I would not give up hope. I prayed every day, three times a day, asking God to show me a miracle. I was using my mind, thinking my son would wake up day and night. I imagined he would wake up and talk to me every day for two months. Before I went to sleep, I would tell my mind my son would wake up. I was using my subconscious mind to *will* my son awake every minute. The doctor was happy with my oldest son's test results. He was okay; there was no damage to the brain, but he was still in a coma.

One day, I prayed to God to show me what kinds of herbs I should drop into my son's mouth, so I started researching the kinds of herbs I should use. I fell asleep one night, and I dreamt about herbs. I dreamt of adaptogens, and I believed they could be used for my son. Adaptogens are non-toxic plants that help the body resist stressors of all kinds, whether physical, chemical, or biological. These herbs and roots have been used for centuries in Chinese and Ayurveda healing traditions. I searched for the herbs and found them in liquid drop form. I ordered them, flew to the Philippines, and I went to see my three sons. The younger two boys were living with a family who was hired by their teacher and social worker to care for them while I stayed with my oldest son in the hospital.

I didn't tell the doctor and the nurses that I was giving the herbs to my son. When I was by his bed, and nobody was watching me, I dropped the herbal supplement into my son's mouth, hoping he would open his eyes. Day and night, I imagined my son opening his eyes and getting out of the hospital bed. When I was alone beside my son's bed, I cried. I wanted him to see me; I did everything I could to save my son. I signed up for more loans to pay the hospital bills, hoping to save my son's life. I knew God would show us a miracle. For a week, I was by his side in the hospital, dropping the herbs in his mouth. I would use just a few drops, only enough to wet his lips. I was not giving up.

After two months of being comatose, he opened his eyes. I was holding his hand, and he started moving a little bit. I was so happy; the miracle had happened. I jumped for joy and called the doctor and nurses. My son was awake! He smiled and started talking to me, his mama. I cried because God is so good all the time, showing me another miracle in my life.

The coma turned into a miracle, joy, and answered prayers. With my subconscious mind, I imagined every day that my son would wake up again and come back to life. I praised God for His mercy and love and for hearing my prayers many times in my life. The description of Dr. Joseph Murphy's book, *The Power of Your Subconscious Mind,* gives a wonderful explanation of the power we have inside ourselves:

Your thoughts and feelings create your destiny. Whatever your conscious and subconscious minds agree upon will come to pass. Think of illness, and you will be ill. Think of happiness, and you will be happy. You have the power to control what goes into your mind. Instead of dwelling on depressing and life-sapping thoughts, feed your subconscious with life-giving patterns, and your actions and reactions will match your thoughts.[12]

I would also like to share some quotes from Dr. Joseph Murphy with you. I think are essential to remember:

- "Just keep your conscious mind busy with expectation of the best."
- "Your desire is your prayer. Picture the fulfillment of your desire new and feel its reality, and you will experience the joy of the answered."
- "Prayer is the soul's sincere desire. Your desire is your prayer. It comes out of your deepest needs, and it reveals the things you want in life."
- "Busy your mind with the concepts of harmony, health, peace, and goodwill and wonders will happen in your life."
- "The only path by which another person can upset you is through your own thought."

Quotes in the Bible that Inspired Me

---

[12] Joseph Murphy, *The Power of Your Subconscious Mind,* (Tarcherperigee: 2009).

In an article called "Bible Verses About Miracles," the Bible Study Tools Staff has compiled a list of Bible verses regarding miracles that It relates to what I shared. I would like to share part of this list here:

When you seek God's presence and request Him to intervene in your situation, you can see miracles happen! God has power over all creation and has the ability to work a miracle for you. The Bible verses below will teach of the miracles Jesus performed as well as how we can have the faith to believe in a miracle.

Acts 3:16

By faith in the name of Jesus, this man whom you see and know was made strong. It is Jesus' name and the faith that comes through him that has completely healed him, as you can all see.

Deuteronomy 10:21

He is the one you praise; he is your God, who performed for you those Great and awesome wonders you saw with your own eyes.

Exodus 15:26

He said, "If you listen carefully to the LORD your God and do what is Right in his eyes, if you pay attention to his commands and keep all his decrees, I will not bring on you any of the diseases I brought on the Egyptians, for I am the LORD, who heals you."

Jeremiah 32:27

"I am the LORD, the God of all mankind. Is anything too hard for me?"

John 2:11

What Jesus did here in Cana of Galilee was the first of the signs through which he revealed his glory; and his disciples believed in him.

Luke 18:27

Jesus replied, "What is impossible with man is possible with God."

Mark 9:23

"'If you can't?'" said Jesus. "Everything is possible for one who believes."

Matthew 17:20

He replied, "Because you have so little faith. Truly, I tell you, if you have faith as small as a mustard seed, you can say to this mountain, 'Move from here to there,' and it will move. Nothing will be impossible for you."

Matthew 19:26

Jesus looked at them and said, "With man, this is impossible, but with God, all things are possible."

Matthew 21:21

Jesus replied, "Truly I tell you, if you have faith and do not doubt, not only can you do what was done to the fig tree, but also you can say to this mountain, 'Go, throw yourself into the sea,' and it will be done."[13]

Just remember, the doctor is dressing the wounds. God is the Healer.

---

[13] BibleStudyTool Staff, "Bible Verses About Miracles," BibleStudyTools.com, last updated February 9, 2021, https://www.biblestudytools.com/topical-verses/bible-verses-about-miracles/.

Chapter 17

Confusion and Hospital Gowns

In 1997, I visited the Philippines for four weeks to see my boys and to give my husband a chance to move to the USA and bring my kids, too. We had an agreement that he would not abuse me, and I would give him another chance because of the advice from my family and the pastor of the church. But after four weeks of staying together, we couldn't get along. We had arguments because he didn't want to come to the USA. He said that I should send him money, and he would live with the boys in the Philippines.

All the visas for my kids were ready, but a babysitter for three boys would be expensive in the USA. I told my husband I would work, and he would stay with the kids, but he didn't want to live in the USA because he had an ex-girlfriend who had come back from Saudi Arabia and was now living in the Philippines. While I was in the USA, he had been living with another woman, even though we were married and had three boys. I was so disappointed again. So, I decided to go back to the USA alone and leave my kids with my husband and family.

Before my return flight to the USA, I needed to get my medical certificate in Manila. Philippine law requires a medical exam before a person can fly to the USA, so I went to the Manila Hospital to get the checkup and certificate before going to the airport. I found out I was pregnant during that visit. "Are you positive?" I asked. The test was positive, though. I flew back to the United States, knowing that I was pregnant with my fourth child. I was worried.

When I arrived in Los Angeles, I called my immigration lawyer and told him the story of what happened during the visit, and he said to just bring my sons to Los Angeles because they had U.S. A visas already, and they could come anytime.

My lawyer filed the paperwork so I could divorce my husband. I was crying to my lawyer because I didn't know what to do. The same lawyer who processed the divorce papers also filed the immigration papers necessary so I could immigrate my sons to the USA. The U.S. immigration office approved my three son's permanent resident applications, so I wanted to bring them to live with me, but it was so expensive to have a babysitter. I was the only one working, and their father didn't want the boys to move. He only wanted the money I was sending; he didn't want the kids. My mom and sister were taking care of the kids—they wanted me to send money to them, too.

I knew my kids were not eating right, and I was worried for their safety. My husband and family members were using the money for something else. But I kept sending the money every month because my three boys are so small. I couldn't sleep thinking of them and their situation, plus I was pregnant again.

When I saw the doctor in the USA, he wanted me to abort the baby or put it up for adoption. I didn't know what to do. I didn't have anyone to ask. I was confused, and it was too much. I began thinking, *how can I work pregnant and then have and take care of another baby?* I prayed, "Lord, give me answers about what to do." Then, the doctor suggested I let him go ahead and abort the baby. He told me he could just remove it as I was only a few weeks along. I said okay and scheduled an appointment for the abortion a week later.

When I arrived, the nurse had me change into a hospital gown and put me on a gurney. While I was in the room at the clinic, I was praying to God about whether I was doing the right thing and had made the right decision. The nurse prepared the injection. I said to the nurse, "I need to go to the bathroom." I was in the gown already, but I was scared to have the procedure. I went to the back door and said, "I need to get something in my car." Then I ran away; I drove my car to go home, still in the hospital gown, because I was afraid to abort my baby. I called the doctor later and begged, "Please give me another week to think. He said Okay, and after one week, the clinic nurse called me. She called me a lot until I agreed to schedule an appointment and come in.

When I was in the clinic, we went through the same process. I needed to put my hospital gown on, and they put me on the gurney. I said again, "I need to get something in the car." And when I got in the car, I prayed. After I prayed, I drove back home. I was so scared. Then the doctor told me, "I will give you one more week, and then you will need to either keep the baby or put it up for adoption." After one week, I knew that would be the last week to abort the baby. I was so confused and worried, and I didn't know what to do.

I called my lawyer because I needed advice. My lawyer advised me to keep the baby and put it up for adoption. But the doctor said I could go through with the abortion, so I needed to come into the clinic. The doctor said this was my last chance to do it. Otherwise, the baby will be significant, and the procedure will not be easy.

I went to the clinic once again. I put on my hospital gown and lay down on the gurney while the nurse prepared the injection. In the room, I saw a tall guy wearing white, and His face was so shiny. He came to me and said, "Get up and go home. Don't do it." He tapped my shoulders three times, and He disappeared.

And when the nurse came back to the room, I said, "No. I want to go home." I ran away from the room, again with the hospital gown on. I drove back home, and I carried my baby until nine months when he was born.

I knew God was protecting me even when my decisions were up and down, and I was confused and very stressed because of my situation. God was still there for me, even when I was struggling in my life.

I kept going, determined not to give up. I wanted to tackle the high mountain of too many problems. Even though it was so complicated and challenging to do, I kept pushing to keep going because of my kids. One night, I could see the light at the end of the tunnel. It was March 20th,^ the night before I gave birth when I dreamed a rainbow was in the sky behind where my kids were standing. There were four boys, smiling and happy together. My kids then told me, "Mom, don't worry. We are all behind you."

Then my youngest son said to me, "Mom, you can do it. Don't give up. You are my hero."

Bible Verses about Bravery

Deuteronomy 31:6

"Be strong and courageous. Do not be afraid or terrified because of them, for the LORD your God goes with you; he will never leave you nor forsake you."

Isaiah 40:29-31

"He gives strength to the weary and increases the power of the weak. Even youths grow tired and weary, and young men stumble and fall, but those who hope in the LORD will renew their strength. They will soar on wings like eagles; they will run and not grow weary; they will walk and not be faint."

Chapter 18
Hot Chocolate and Court in Los Angeles

I was twenty-eight years old on time. I had just returned from the Philippines two days before, and I needed to go back to work at the Pomona Hospital in California. I was so mad with myself, so discouraged, and faced so much discouragement in my life. The non-stop problems, just one after another, made it so I couldn't sleep.

Sometimes, I would think about not waking up, but I had my kids to think about. They were so small and needed their mother. One day, I was lying down on the bed, and I did not get up. I kept crying and lying there. When I went to work later that day, my co-worker asked me why my eyes were swollen. I explained to her that I had been crying because of my non-stop problems. She said, "You must be happy to have seen your kids, and you just had a vacation. What happened? Why don't you bring your kids?" All I could reply was that my husband was not ready to come to the USA, but I was not going to tell her I was pregnant again.

My co-worker was a Hispanic lady, and she was so lovely to me, like a sister. She would love to give me food she prepared, and I shared my smoothie with her when we were working together. The hospital had appointed me to train her. She had just graduated from school, and she was acting as my assistant while I taught her physical therapy.

My co-worker invited me to attend her baby girl's birthday party at her home. She told me to come after I was finished with work. She didn't work that day because she needed to prepare for her daughter's birthday. The day of the party, she called me after work. She told me to come to her house; she said she would be waiting for me. Since she lived close to my apartment, only a few blocks away on Alvarado Street in Los Angeles, I decided to go to it.

I told her, "Okay, yes, I'll come just to see your daughter for her birthday. I can only stay for thirty minutes because I have work to early the next day".

She said, "Okay, just eat and go home, that's all."

When I arrived at her home, there were plenty of people in her house. I didn't know anyone; I only knew her parents and children, that's all. I was outside sitting where the tables had been set up when my co-worker motioned for me to come get some food. I said, "Okay." She introduced me to a male friend of hers and told him to get me a cup of hot chocolate. My friend brought me a plate of food, and the man handed me the Styrofoam cup of hot chocolate. I started drinking the hot chocolate before I ate, and I began to feel dizzy. I don't know what happened to me after feeling lightheaded. The last thing I remember was drinking the hot chocolate. That's all.

The following day, when my friend went to work, I wasn't there. So, she kept calling me to find out why I wasn't at work. When she arrived home after work that early evening, she noticed my car was parked on the street near her house, in the same place it was the night before.

I woke up in the hospital the next day. I asked the nurse, "Why am I here in the hospital?"

The nurse replied, "The police brought you to the L.A. Hospital today."

I asked, "Why? What happened? Why was I passed out?"

The nurse said, "You need to talk to a social worker. You were raped last night."

"Who raped me?" I asked.

She explained to me, "The police brought you to the hospital. The manager of the hotel called the police because noon was checkout time at the hotel, and you didn't answer the door. When the motel management and police opened the door to the room. You were on the floor, vomiting and bleeding, and the police brought you to the hospital.

The nurse then told me I was pregnant (which I already knew) and had been raped by two men because the specimen results showed two different samples. The hotel manager gave the police a copy of the surveillance video from the previous night. The video showed that two men brought me to the hotel that night, and I wasn't walking straight. Then, they checked into the hotel room.

The Los Angeles police came back to the hospital to talk to me. I told the police that I was at my friend's house for her baby's birthday party. I parked my car near her home. Hadn't eaten any food that night, but the man handed me a hot chocolate to drink. I explained that was all I remembered.

I asked the police if they could check to see who had checked me into the hotel. The manager had given them the name of the person as he paid with a credit or debit card. The police immediately began looking for the men who raped me. I didn't know who they were, but they had the name of the hotel.

Again, I was sad with my life and the ongoing trials and non-stop problems. I prayed to God, "Why me?" But then I said to God, "Forgive me because you saved me and my baby." I was confused and worried. I wanted to abort the baby or just go to sleep and never wake up. I kept crying non-stop. When I was almost ready to give up, God showed me His peace while I was reading the Bible. The words of God were the only source of strength I had; I had no family or husband to cry to. I didn't share any of my problems with anyone; I kept them to myself.

I managed to continue to fight harder and not give up because of my precious boys. They were my strength to keep going, even though things were so hard for me and them. The boys were young and had no one else to turn to except me. We needed each other.

When I slept, I would cry to God, who gave me courage, comfort, and peace in my heart. Since I was a child, there were so many challenges in my life. There was no end to the trials that would fill me up almost until I couldn't breathe, but the most remarkable thing I had was God, who cared and still cares for me and my kids.

It is not easy when you become discouraged when your faith is tested, like the story of Abraham in the Bible. He was tried by God through his son Isaac when Abraham was told to bring Isaac to an altar to give him as an offering to God. Obedient, Abraham tied his only son Isaac to an altar to sacrifice him to the Lord.

I know our problems and trials are nothing compared to those of Jesus. He died on the cross for our sins, He suffered for our mistakes, He saved us from our unrighteousness to save our souls. At that moment, my trials were nothing to God, but God can give us more strength to trust He completely and humbled our hearts to God.

The police investigation lasted eight months, and they found one of the two men who raped me. They caught him and put him in jail. I didn't know the other person, and he was still free. He hadn't given a name at the hotel, so he was still in hiding. The man who was arrested also wouldn't provide the name of the second man to the police. I didn't know the man who the police had captured, but I noticed he was the one who had given me the hot chocolate that night. They had found drugs in my system, and it was determined that the man had put them in my hot chocolate.

By now, my stomach was getting big, and it was almost time to give birth. I wanted to abort my baby because of my situation; it was too much, and I faced unstoppable trials. I couldn't bear it anymore. I was confused.

The hearing was held at the Los Angeles courthouse. It was a hassle for me to make every court date because I was working, and by this time, my son had been born, so I also had a tiny baby to care for. It was so exhausting, tiring, and stressful. I was so mad with my life. I was so frustrated, and sometimes I said, "God, why did you allow this to happen to me?" The only encouragement I had was seeing my newborn son smiling at me. And he smiled all the time!

I never spoke to my family about what was going on in my life. When I told my lawyer about the court case, he said to me, "What a life you've had full of troubles, non-stop, one after another."

I said to my lawyer, "I don't know why. I was born to suffer, and God keeps punishing me all the time, my whole life."

My attorney was an older gentleman, and he was the only person I felt safe with and could tell my sad stories. There was no break. The trials just kept going. I wished my mom and dad had killed me when I was a child so I didn't need to suffer this miserable life.

The court hearing took two years. I was so tired of traveling back and forth to Los Angeles, my home, and work; it was a 45-minute drive each way. Finding a parking spot in downtown L.A. was difficult because the cost of parking a car was expensive. To add to my troubles, I needed to be absent from work during the day to attend court when it was in session. The judge wanted to wait for the other person who raped me to be arrested, but they only had one man in jail, so the trial proceeded.

In the last hearing, the man on trial was found guilty, and the judge sentenced him to ten to fifteen years in prison, five years of community service, and imposed a fine. The judge implemented an order of protection for me and my son until he was eighteen years old. The judge also ordered me to have a gun so that I could carry it with me to protect myself and my son. But I told the judge that I didn't want to take a gun because I was afraid to have one. I told him that my son and I would be fine and thanked God we were safe. God was watching over us. I also thanked God for giving me justice in my case.

The court hearings were final, and I had survived. I never shared this story with anyone until now. During the two years, I began dreaming about the men who raped me. I decided I needed to forgive them and, specifically, the one who was found guilty of rape. I went to the court and told the judge to lower the man's jail sentence. I told the judge I had forgiven my rapist because my son and I were safe. God had been watching over us. The judge agreed to grant my petition because I had ignored the man. His sentence was lowered to five years in prison and five years of community service.

My life had been horrible, a story no one could imagine. But God knows everything, and God is still with my boys and me today, protecting us.

Bible Verses about Strength

Deuteronomy 20:4

"For the LORD your God is the one who goes with you to fight for you against your enemies to give you victory."

Psalm 119:28

"My soul is weary with sorrow; strengthen me according to your word."

1 Chronicles 16:11

"Look to the LORD and his strength; seek his face always."

2 Timothy 1:7

"For the Spirit God gave us does not make us timid, but gives us power, love and self-discipline."

1 Corinthians 16:13

"Be on your guard; stand firm in the faith; be courageous; be strong."

2 Corinthians 1:7

"And our hope for you is firm because we know that just as you share in our sufferings, so also you share in our comfort."

Isaiah 40:29

"He gives strength to the weary and increases the power of the weak."

2 Thessalonians 3:2

"And pray that we may be delivered from wicked and evil people, for not everyone has faith."

Isaiah 41:10

"So do not fear, for I am with you; do not be dismayed, for I am your God. I will strengthen you and help you; I will uphold you with my righteous right hand."

John 16:33

"I have told you these things so that in me you may have peace. In this world, you will need help. But take heart! I have overcome the world."

Joshua 1:9

"Have I not commanded you? Be strong and courageous. Do not be afraid; do not be discouraged, for the LORD your God will be with you wherever you go."

Philippians 4:13

"I can do all this through him who gives me strength."

Psalm 27:1

"The LORD is my light and my salvation—whom shall I fear? The LORD is the stronghold of my life—of whom shall I be afraid?"

Psalm 29:11

"The LORD gives strength to his people; the LORD blesses his people with peace."

Psalm 73:26

"My flesh and my heart may fail, but God is the strength of my heart and my portion forever."

Psalm 18:1-2

"I love you, LORD, my strength. The LORD is my rock, my fortress, and my deliverer; my God is my rock, in whom I take refuge, my shield and the horn of my salvation, my stronghold."

Ephesians 6:10

"Finally, be strong in the Lord and in his mighty power."

Isaiah 40:31

"But those who hope in the LORD will renew their strength. They will soar on wings like eagles; they will run and not grow weary; they will walk and not be faint."

Mark 12:30

"Love the Lord your God with all your heart and with all your soul and with all your mind and with all your strength."

2 Corinthians 12:9-10

"But he said to me, 'My grace is sufficient for you, for my power is made perfect in weakness.' Therefore, I will boast all the more gladly about my weaknesses so that Christ's power may rest on me. That is why, for Christ's sake, I delight in weaknesses, in insults, in hardships, in persecutions, in difficulties. For when I am weak, then I am strong."

Psalm 46:1

"God is our refuge and strength, an ever-present help in trouble."

Nehemiah 8:10

"Nehemiah said, 'Go and enjoy choice food and sweet drinks, and send some to those who have nothing prepared. This day is holy to our Lord. Do not grieve, for the joy of the LORD is your strength.'"

Psalm 22:19

"But you, LORD, do not be far from me. You are my strength; come quickly to help me."

Psalm 28:7-8

"The LORD is my strength and my shield; my heart trusts in him, and he helps me. My heart leaps for joy, and with my song, I praise him. The LORD is the strength of his people, a fortress of salvation for his anointed one."

Psalm 118:14

"The LORD is my strength and my defense; he has become my salvation."

Isaiah 12:2

"Surely God is my salvation; I will trust and not be afraid. The LORD, the LORD himself is my strength and my defense; he has become my salvation."

Isaiah 33:2

"LORD, be gracious to us; we long for you. Be our strength every morning, our salvation in time of distress."

Isaiah 40:29-31

"He gives strength to the weary and increases the power of the weak. Even youths grow tired and weary, and young men stumble and fall, but those who hope in the LORD will renew their strength. They will soar on wings like eagles; they will run and not grow weary; they will walk and not be faint."

Habakkuk 3:19

"The Sovereign LORD is my strength; he makes my feet like the feet of a deer; he enables me to tread on the heights."

Ephesians 3:16

"I pray that out of his glorious riches, he may strengthen you with power through his Spirit in your inner being…"

1 Peter 4:11

"If anyone speaks, they should do so as one who speaks the very words of God. If anyone serves, they should do so with the strength God provides so that in all things, God may be praised through Jesus Christ. To him be the glory and the power forever and ever. Amen."

Chapter 19

A Baby Born on the Freeway

The morning after my dream in which my son and soon-to-be-born son had spoken to me, I was in Los Angeles at my friend's home. I was pregnant at any time, and I was cleaning my friend's house, cooking, and shopping at a few markets. My doctor had advised me not to go too far because the baby was due soon, but I wanted to see my friend because she had been on vacation from work for a few months, and we hadn't seen each other in a while. So, I decided to make the trip from where I lived in North Hollywood to Los Angeles.

While I was visiting with her, I felt that the baby was on the way. I called my doctor, who was in the Granada Hills Valley Hospital. When I called and told him I was near downtown Los Angeles, he said to have someone drive me to the hospital and not contact the paramedics because they would take me to the nearest hospital, not the hospital where he worked. I called a taxi, but the taxi didn't come quickly; I waited twenty minutes. Finally, I knocked on the door of the manager of the apartment where my friend lived, told them the situation, and the husband and wife agreed to drive me to the hospital.

It was a busy time on the freeway, around 6:30 p.m., and we had to speed because my water broke already. I was sitting in the back seat, and I told the apartment manager, who also was friends with my friend, that I was going to push and that the baby was coming out. He feared that I would have the baby in the car, so he was driving at ninety miles per hour. Then, a single police car started following us, which scared the landlord more, so he began driving one hundred miles per hour. The police called for police backup, and we now had three police officers following the car and telling us to pull over.

We never pulled over, and I later learned that they believed we may be running drugs. I was holding the baby by the head as we drove to the hospital; by this time, the baby was already halfway out, so I told the man to just pull over. The police were so mad when we finally pulled over to the side of the freeway (SR-170 in Los Angeles). The officer knocked on my door in the backseat, and I rolled down the window. I said to him, "I'm having a baby. I'm holding my baby's head."

The police officer told the other officers to give us an escort to the hospital. We had a police escort on either side of the car, with another police car in front of us so the other cars on the freeway would get out of our way. We drove faster and faster because I had pushed my baby out already.

When we arrived at the hospital, the officer took his t-shirt off and wrapped it around the baby, but the placenta was still not coming out. He helped carry me to the gurney, and I asked him his name. He answered Joshua and I said, "Thank you for saving me and my baby." When I got in the delivery room, he just disappeared.

I knew he was an angel who had carried my son and covered him with his t-shirt.

At that time, I was the only one giving birth in that hospital, so all the nurses and doctors were helping me. It took me forty-five minutes to deliver the baby while on the freeway, and when I was in the delivery room, the placenta came out. The doctor was worried because the baby did not cry, and something that looked like plastic was covering his eyes and nose. It was unusual and seldom is a baby covered with a plastic-like substance. The doctor cut the plastic, turned my baby upside down, and the newborn started to cry. Then, the doctor announced the baby was a boy, and I was crying because the ultrasounds looked as if the child was a girl, but he came out as a boy. After my son's first cry, all he did was smile at me and everyone else.

The doctor suggested that I put the baby up for adoption because of my situation. A babysitter in the city would be expensive, and I still had my three boys back in the Philippines. But when he smiled at me, I told the doctor that I would think about it. I knew it would be difficult, but I prayed to God to help me survive again.

I thanked God for the blessing of delivering the baby on freeway SR-170 in Los Angeles. I named him Joshua, named after the policeman who chased us on the freeway and then escorted us to the hospital. The entire event was a blessing. Everything turned into blessings and miracles. God sent angels to rescue me, and God protected the driver, his wife, my son, and me from any accident while we were speeding. I praise God for everything and His love and mercy.

Quotes on Joy and Happiness

"Every day, in every way, I am getting happier and happier."

"Happiness is my birthright. I choose to be happy, and I deserve to be happy."

"Every new day starts with happiness, is full of joy, and ends with contentment."

"Happiness is contagious. I spread happiness to others and absorb happiness from others."

"I touch many lives. My happiness makes all these people happy, thus making it one big happy world."

"My happy disposition attracts happiness into my life. I interact only with happy people and have only happy experiences."

"The whole process of living makes me happy. Moving towards my goal makes me happy."

"I am grateful to God for this wonderful life. I am thankful to everybody who has touched my life and made it worth living."

"I enjoy every moment of the day. Be happy is my motto."

"Being happy comes easy to me. Happiness is my second nature."

"Happy thoughts come to me naturally. I always land in happy circumstances."

Quotes in the Bible about Joy and Happiness

Psalm 118:24 ESV

"This is the day that the Lord has made; let us rejoice and be glad in it."

Psalm 30:5 NKJV

"Weeping may endure for a night, but joy comes in the morning."

John 15:11

"I have told you this so that my joy may be in you and that your joy may be complete."

Nehemiah 8:10

"For the joy of the Lord is your strength."

Psalm 34:17 NKJV

"The righteous cry out, the Lord hears, and delivers them out of all their troubles." God will make a way even when there seems to be no way.

Isaiah 26:3

"You will keep in perfect peace those whose minds are steadfast because they trust in you."

Numbers 6:24 ESV

"The Lord bless you and keep you."

Numbers 6:25 ESV

"The Lord make His face shine upon you and be gracious to you."

Numbers 6:26 ESV

"The Lord lifts His countenance upon you and gives you peace."

Romans 8:28

"And we know that in all things God works for the good of those who love him, who have been called according to his purpose."

Chapter 20
Miracle Patient

A month after giving birth to my son Joshua, I went back to work at the Pomona Hospital in California, as a Physical Therapist. I was worried about my three sons in the Philippines—James, seven years old, and Joel six years old. And Abraham, five years old. I had to work very hard to support them and Joshua, who was in the USA with me. I had to start leaving Joshua with a babysitter at only one-month-old.

I would leave my son with the babysitter for twelve to twenty-four hours sometimes. I was crying every day at how hard it was to go to work, go home, do some errands, and never have enough time for Joshua. When I would drop my baby off with the babysitter, he was sleeping, and then when I would come back from work at midnight to pick him up, he was asleep. I never saw him awake because I dropped him off early in the morning and picked him up around midnight. Sometimes, I needed to work two jobs and overtime because the babysitter was so expensive, and I needed to support my three boys in the Philippines and my whole family. I was acting as a single parent, a mother and father to all the boys, and supporting my entire family because no one else worked. Being a single parent was not the most straightforward job in the world, but it was the best job you could ever imagine.

I was so exhausted working two jobs and had no time for myself, mainly because no one was supporting me. I had no time to rest. The only day I had off was Saturday, and I would go to church, and that was the only time I had with my son. Sunday, I worked another job, and it was so difficult for me every day. I would cry because I wanted to give up. Sometimes, I prayed to the Lord to *take* me and my kids because I was so tired and didn't want to worry anymore.

Sometimes, my prayers to God were about why my life was full of pain. Why was my life so full of miseries? My entire life had been complicated and full of hardships. I had faced non-stop hardships with no breaks from childhood to high school to adulthood, even when I was married with kids. Ever since elementary school, I only slept three hours a night. I would ask God why He would give me this. It was too much of a burden, and I had been born into suffering. My problems felt overwhelming and never-ending.

I came to realize that God was always there with me. I survived when I was a child; I stayed when I was in elementary school, high school, and college; I survived through my marriage and now with four boys. When I was so downtrodden and exhausted, I would just cry to God. When I would drive, I would put on Christian songs and turn the music up loud to make me relax, and I would just sing. I was praying to God to give me comfort and peace. I still believed one day I would be over this calvary.

I read these texts in the Bible:

- "So do not fear, for I am with you; do not be dismayed, for I am your God. I will strengthen you and help you; I will uphold you with my righteous right hand" (Isa. 41:10 NIV).
- "The Lord is my strength and my defense; he has become my salvation. Shouts of joy and victory resound in the tents of the righteous: 'The Lord's right hand has done mighty things! The Lord's right hand is lifted high; the Lord's right hand has done mighty things!'" (Ps. 118:14-16 NIV).
- "For the Spirit God gave us does not make us timid, but gives us power, love, and self-discipline" (2 Tim. 1:7 NIV).

After I read these verses in the Bible, I cried loudly to God. When I was driving, I asked God, "When will these non-stop problems be done in my life?"

Then, I found another way to put my problems aside for a few hours. I decided to attend classes on alternative medicine and natural food medicine. The private classes were four hours in length, three times a week in Los Angeles, so during those times, I forgot all my worries and problems.

Also, on Saturdays after church, I would visit my patients in the nursing home so I could have a relaxed time with them and give them free massage therapy. This also kept my mind occupied, and I didn't think about my problems for a while. Sometimes, I would bring Josh to visit the patients who were depressed. I would sing, and my son would start smiling at the patients; this was our hobby.

They enjoyed it, and I could relax doing this small thing for them because if I had been home, I would've cried.

One day, I prayed to God and said, "I have four boys, three in the Philippines and one in the USA. My mind is shattered over working with no rest and no sleep. There was just work, fatigue, exhaustion, and non-stop problems." But I never gave up praying. I never quit and just kept praying to God. I saw the light at the end of the tunnel. There was a rainbow, and one day, all this would be over.

When I read the Bible, I cried to God, who was my only hope, and He gave me courage and strength. When my baby Joshua started smiling and laughing, I felt safe and motivated to keep going on my journey. I didn't want to give up just because I didn't have a husband or family to share my life stories or my hardships with. I didn't even tell my friends about what I was going through. There was only God.

I cried to God every night because I was worried about my three boys in the Philippines, and my mind was so scattered because my situation was so much to bear. My pathway was very dark. I had no life and no light, and things were always getting darker and darker with no sunshine. I prayed to God to put me and my sons to *sleep*, so we didn't have to worry anymore. I would cry and cry and cry until my pillowcase was wet. If I could count my tears, there would be too many to even put into containers.

I missed my boys. I didn't get to see Joshua as much as I wanted. Sometimes, I wouldn't see him all day or for multiple days. My other three sons were thousands of miles away from me. I wanted to be with them.

One day, I said to God, "Help, can you give me a job where I can bring my son to work?" The following day, I went to work and saw a patient who was ninety-five years old. I called him Mr. Grandpa. Grandpa is a term of endearment used in the Philippines for the elderly. He'd had a stroke and was left totally paralyzed in half his body. Couldn't eat and was on a liquid diet. But his brain had remained well; he had not lost his marbles and had a very sharp sense of humor.

This day was the last day of his physical therapy. He asked me to come to work with him as his private caregiver, where I would live in his home and provide him with physical therapy. I told him I couldn't because I had a contract with the hospital and explained that I needed this work because of my personal and family situation. I also explained that I had a three-month-old son who lived with me. I knew I wouldn't be able to manage helping him, my job at the hospital, and my second job.

Since the patient needed to go home, his lawyer called me. He asked if I could work an outpatient job because the patient would like me to provide therapy for him. I explained it would be too hard for me as I was already doing too much, so I couldn't accept the extra work. But the old man really wanted me to work for him, so he called his doctor at the hospital where I worked and asked if I could at least work with him temporarily.

The doctor who hired me at the hospital said it was okay for me to work for Mr. Grandpa. So, Mr. Grandpa's attorney made the arrangements for me to go work for him. The doctor thought the man would pass soon because he was only drinking Ensure drinks, had suffered a stroke, and had prostate cancer, so the doctor predicted I would stay with him at the most six months. The doctor wanted me to be sure he was drinking the Ensure drinks and was taking his medicine. Then, when he passed, I would come back to the hospital.

After this, I agreed to talk to Mr. Grandpa and his lawyer. I told them that the problem with being a live-in caretaker was that I had a tiny baby who was three months old. I couldn't live with him, so I refused the job. Mr. Grandpa didn't want to hire anyone else, so he told me that I could bring my son with me to live with him as well. He said that I could move in and then just take care of him and my son. He agreed to also give me one day off a week, on Saturday. With this offer, I wouldn't need a babysitter anymore. So, Mr. Grandpa, his lawyer, and I all agreed to the terms. When I went home, I thanked God for answering my prayers.

When I moved in with Mr. Grandpa, he said, "I have a library in my home. I have plenty of healing books. You can study about health in all the books that are in my home." While in the hospital, the old man noticed me drinking a smoothie every time I gave him therapy. I would drink them because I didn't have time to cook for myself, so I would drink a smoothie for lunch or breakfast.

Mr. Grandpa said to me, "I want to live up to one hundred years old.

I asked, "How?"

Mr. Grandpa said, "I don't want to drink Ensure; it is too sweet." He told me I needed to create my own formula for his food, from seeds, nuts, vegetables, fruits, and herbs. Then he would drink that, not Ensure. He said he would give me two weeks to study and create a formula for his food: seeds, nuts, vegetables, fruits, herbs, vitamins, minerals, and other foods. He believed in me and saw something in me that I didn't see in myself. He wanted to live until he was one hundred years old. On that night, I asked for wisdom from above on how to do it. It was not an easy task, but I was happy because I had my baby son Joshua was with me, so I wanted to do this for him. I was also excited to do this because I wanted to learn more about healthy foods, and studying about them was one of my favorite things to do.

After two weeks, I created a formula called Miracle Mix. I would make this powerful Miracle Mix smoothie for his breakfast, lunch, and dinner. I made it from all different kinds of fruits and vegetables. I added seeds and various nuts, plus his favorite herbs. I ordered a couple good juicers and blenders to help make the smoothies. I would drink the smoothies with Mr. Grandpa. I sometimes ate fish and rice as well, but most of our food and nourishment was found in the smoothies.

There was a system for the smoothies. Every meal was a different color smoothie. The morning or breakfast smoothie was green, with kale as the main ingredient. The lunch drink was yellow, and its color came from various fruits, while the dinner smoothie had a red color because of beets and other red fruits and vegetables.

I gave him therapy and exercise every day. I would drive us to the beach because we lived near the water. I would have my son on my back in a child carrier while I pushed Mr. Grandpa's wheelchair. I took Mr. Grandpa, wherever I went, to the market or to church, because he didn't want me to take a day off. I was busy taking care of a stroke patient and a tiny baby. I drove all the time between his office and his other homes in Malibu, Beverly Hills, and Santa Barbara. We would just pick up his mail. Every day, there were lots of jobs for me, but I was so happy to have my baby Joshua with me and to be able to take care of him at the same time I was working. It was a blessing and answered prayer.

Every month, we visited his doctor for his appointment, and the nurse was surprised by how the older man was doing. Mr. Grandpa was more alert and had more energy. Also, the results of his blood sugar and blood pressure tests were becoming regular. At his appointment three months into my care, his bloodwork showed he was getting better, and his cancer was in remission. The doctor also noticed Mr. Grandpa no longer looked like a dying person. I stayed quiet and didn't tell the doctor what I was doing in giving the elderly man the Miracle Mix smoothies I'd created for him. I just listened to my patient's wish to live to one hundred years old.

The doctor asked what I was doing with him, and I explained that Mr. Grandpa hadn't wanted to drink the Ensure drinks because they were too sweet. I made him raw juice for his food every day because I created my own formula. Plus, Mr. Grandpa had faith that God would let him live longer, he was getting more exercise, and my son was smiling at him every day.

The doctor was shocked at what I told him. He recognized Mr. Grandpa had a strong determination to fight. It had reached the point where I helped him practice using his walker, and he was able to eat soft, healthy foods. At six months in my care, the doctor noticed Mr. Grandpa's blood pressure had improved. He ordered me not to give the older man the blood pressure medication when his blood pressure was normal, only if it was high. I needed to monitor his blood pressure and sugar moving forward.

When I would work in the kitchen, cooking and cleaning, I would put Joshua in his baby crib and let him watch Bible story videos. He and Mr. Grandpa would watch them together. At about four months old, Joshua didn't want the milk in his bottle anymore. He wouldn't drink it, and I was worried because he would cry since he didn't like it. My son would always sit at the table with Mr. Grandpa while we ate, watching what we did every day. One day, he pointed to the smoothie Mr. Grandpa was drinking, so I decided to let him try it. He enjoyed it, and from then on, Joshua would eat what we ate: raw juice smoothies, only drinking milk at night.

When my son started walking at eight months old, he began to help me around the house every morning. He went to Mr. Grandpa in the morning and gave him the newspaper and his cane. He would push the walker over to Mr. Grandpa and open the curtains. Josh did this until he was five. Mr. Grandpa was thrilled with my son. I would put my son in his highchair at the table, and they would drink their smoothies together.

Mr. Grandpa was sharp and active. He asked his doctor if he could travel by airplane, and the doctor agreed if my son and I went along. We traveled to Hawaii, visiting Maui and Honolulu on his private jet and pilot regularly. Mr. Grandpa had a condominium in Hawaii, and we loved it there. I would drive all over Maui, from one end to the other, with Joshua and Mr. Grandpa. We traveled all the time and enjoyed it. We were having fun together. We would stay for a month before traveling back to California.

My son grew up in the car and traveled with Mr. Grandpa until he was five years old and went to school. Joshua started kindergarten, and I continued feeding him the healthy foods I usually did. He would have a smoothie for lunch and fish, rice, corn, green peas, green apple, and banana. The teachers noticed Josh would often drink a smoothie for lunch, and they asked me why JOSHUA was on a diet and was sick. I laughed and told them he wasn't.

Josh had gotten so used to drinking these smoothies that he didn't know how to eat junk food. The class had a party, and he didn't eat the hamburgers or hot dogs. Joshua started drinking his smoothie instead. He just didn't eat junk food or drink soda. The teachers learned from Joshua began to eat and drink healthier things. It was a blessing that the whole school noticed how my son ate.

I needed to take a vacation to visit my sons in the Philippines. I only needed two weeks. I got someone to relieve me of Mr. Grandpa's duties, and I left Josh with a daycare teacher in Glendale. Mr. Grandpa was worried when I went to travel to the Philippines to see my three boys. He didn't like the person who was assigned to care for him in my absence. After I left, Grandpa became dehydrated, and the other caretaker had to take him to the hospital. He wouldn't drink the Ensures the new caretaker gave him because he wanted my smoothies. He was waiting in the hospital for me to return.

When I came back from the Philippines, I went to visit Mr. Grandpa in the hospital with my son Joshua. Because Joshua had grown up with him for the first five years of his life, he and Mr. Grandpa had missed each other so much. Joshua kept smiling at Mr. Grandpa, and they talked so much after being two weeks apart.

Mr. Grandpa had stayed in the hospital while I was gone, and he was ready to go home. Mr. Grandpa told me he was happy with us as his family because he had no children at all. I was delighted, too. Most of his relatives had already died; the only surviving relative was a nephew. His wife had died before he had his stroke. It was a fantastic journey, and God answered my prayers and wishes to take care of my son while I was working.

Mr. Grandpa told me I needed to share my formula with others because it could help lots of people who faced malnutrition. He told me to look specifically at poor countries. I promised Mr. Grandpa I would share them with people around the world.

Mr. Grandpa wished to live to one hundred years old, and he did. He died peacefully and happily at one hundred. Before he died, I told Mr. Grandpa, I was so thankful for him. I said, "I'm grateful to God and to you because you gave me the courage to fight on my journey, and I've been able to have my son with me." My baby Joshua and I missed Mr. Grandpa so much.

Mr. Grandpa had done so much for me. He taught me to fight against the hard life. Taught me to keep going, not to give up, and not to get discouraged. He encouraged me to discover my own healthy formula, which became my own product. He taught me how to sell my products. He taught me to be patient and humble and not be discouraged by my trials. He taught me to make healthy food. He taught me to be a stronger person. He taught me to become a good person. He taught me how to become an excellent example to others. He taught me to be a loveable person.

Mr. Grandpa told me and my kids that we would succeed someday. We only needed to not give up no matter what and have faith and belief. For five years, my son Joshua and I had a great time with Mr. Grandpa. We were all on a journey together from 1998 to 2002. I praise God because He was always there by my son's and my side.

Bible Verses that Inspired Me

Nehemiah 8:10

"...Do not grieve, for the joy of the Lord is your strength."

Isaiah 41:10

"So do not fear, for I am with you; do not be dismayed, for I am your God. I will strengthen you and help you; I will uphold you with my righteous right hand."

Exodus 15:2 NLT

"The Lord is my strength and my song; he has given me victory."

Philippians 4:8

"Finally, brothers and sisters, whatever is true, whatever is noble, whatever is right, whatever is pure, whatever is lovely, whatever is admirable—if anything is excellent or praiseworthy—think about such things."

Colossians 3:1-2

"Since, then, you have been raised with Christ, set your hearts on things above, where Christ is, seated at the right hand of God. Set your minds on things above, not on earthly things."

Psalm 19:14

"May these words of my mouth and this meditation of my heart be pleasing in your sight, Lord, my Rock, and my Redeemer."

Chapter 21

The Building and Rainbows

In 2002, after spending five years with Mr. Grandpa, he died peacefully. My life would change. After his passing, my life continued to be full of obstacles and non-stop trials and troubles, bouncing between small joys and painful problems from one story to another.

I needed to look for a job again, and I decided to go back to the hospital. I applied at Cedar Sinai Hospital in Los Angeles, and I was accepted right away. During my first trip to Los Angeles, I saw the building I had dreamed of when I was a child with the rainbow behind the big building. Now, I passed through downtown Los Angeles every day in the early morning and again in the afternoon, and my dream was a reality.

Having worked at Cedar Sinai for a few months, I had one physical therapy patient who was very sick with cancer. When he was ready to be discharged from the hospital, he asked me if I could visit him privately and provide physical therapy in his home near Venice Beach, California. I loved to work one-on-one with patients, so I accepted the job. I quit the hospital because I not only liked individual patient care, but I also had time for my son. I started working for the man, but he passed away after just a few months.

As I provided physical therapy for him, I also worked with his wife because she was in an accident and broke her femur. The lady was seventy-six years old when I started working with her. I would work with her during the day and then go home to my son. She wanted to meet my son, so I would let him visit. Sometimes, she would travel with me to drop my son off at school. Occasionally, we also saw her after church, and we would go to the beach because she lived by Venice Beach. I cared for her for eight years until she passed away.

When I went home in the evenings, I would drive past the building in my childhood dream. Sometimes, there would be a rainbow shining behind it. It made me happy because I was living my dream. My childhood dream had become a reality. I thanked God for bringing me to this place, but I still could not understand why I was facing so many trials and why my life was like this. I wondered, *why is my life like a rainbow of dark colors?* When I saw the sunrise, I was happy; when I saw the sunset, I was sad.

I couldn't help but ask why? Why did I face so many obstacles in my life? So many trials? So much pain? So many tears? So much sadness? So many deaths that were still raw in my life? So much hardship? So many bad memories? So many troubles? So many problems? So many bad experiences? There were so many disappointments in my life. My life was entirely of discouraging trials.

When I saw the rainbow behind the building, I changed my thinking. I began counting the blessings rather than my problems. I turned to God. God, with His unconditional love and mercy, showed me every day was a miracle.

Bible Verses that Inspired Me

Luke 6:38

"Give, and it will be given to you. A good measure, pressed down, shaken together, and running over, will be poured in your lap. For with the measure you use, it will be measured to you."

Genesis 9:11, 16

"'I establish my covenant with you: Never again will all life be destroyed by the waters of a flood; never again will there be a flood to destroy the earth. . . Whenever the rainbow appears in the clouds, I will see it and remember the everlasting covenant between God and all living creatures of every kind on the earth.'"

Psalm 103:2 NKJV

"Bless the LORD, O my soul, and forget not all his benefits."

Ephesians 5:20 ESV

"Giving thanks always and for everything to God the Father in the name of our Lord Jesus Christ."

Psalm 105:1 ESV

"Oh, give thanks to the LORD; call upon his name; make known his deeds among the peoples!"

Psalm 116:12 ESV

"What shall I render to the LORD for all his benefits to me?"

1 Thessalonians 5:16-18 ESV

"Rejoice always, pray without ceasing, give thanks in all circumstances; for this is the will of God in Christ Jesus for you."

2 Corinthians 9:8

"And God is able to bless you abundantly, so that in all things at all times, having all you need, you will abound in every good work."

Philippians 4:6-7

"Do not be anxious about anything, but in every situation, by Prayer and petition, with thanksgiving, present your requests to God. And the peace of God, which transcends all understanding, will guard your hearts and your minds in Christ Jesus."

Jeremiah 17:7-8

"But blessed is the one who trusts in the LORD, whose confidence is in him. They will be like a tree planted by the water that sends out its roots by the stream. It does not fear when heat comes; its leaves are always green. It has no worries in a year of drought and never fails to bear fruit."

John 1:16

"Out of his fullness, we have all received grace in place of grace already given."

Chapter 22
Single Motorcycle and Bank Miracle

In 2005, I was ready to bring my three sons to the USA. I went back to Manila, Philippines, to pick them up and complete the process of getting their visas. My boys were to have an interview and a physical exam before they could move to the USA. I was bringing the boys to the U.S. Because I wanted to get them away from the abuse of their dad and my family. I needed protection as well, so their father wouldn't block us from flying back to the USA.

I brought all the documents with me to the Philippines. My lawyer had arranged everything in the USA. I only needed to have the embassy stamp the visa, get the passports, have the interview and the physical exam of my sons. Everything was paid for, and I even had my kids' tickets bought. I had already enrolled my three boys in a school close to where I lived, so when they arrived, they could start school immediately.

I had many expenses and debts because of my three sons' hospital bills and my roundtrip tickets so I could visit my son when he was comatose. I was so exhausted and tired because I was supporting my four sons by myself. I was so mad at my family and ex-husband for abusing the kids and stealing the money I sent that was supposed to be used to care for them.

When I flew to the Philippines, I had only enough money for my boys and I am to stay in the hotel plus any expenses for ten days.

My lawyer said I wouldn't have to pay at the embassy. I only needed to show the documents and the passports. The U.S. embassy would stamp my son's visas for their green cards.

After their physical exams on Friday, my kids' interviews for their visas would take place. Our flight to the USA was scheduled to leave on Sunday. We were waiting in line for our visa interview. It required me to have an interview, too, because I was the petitioner of my kids. When we reached the front of the line, I showed the documents and the passports, and the cashier said to me I needed to pay again for the visa. I asked why because my lawyer had paid for everything; I showed her all the receipts from the USA. And the lady cashier said, "No, you need to pay again."

I explained my situation to her. I didn't have any money because I had paid for everything already—the visa, the plane tickets, my sons' hospital bills—I had less than five hundred dollars left in my account. I only had ten days off my job because I had already been back and forth so many times to visit my son, who was in a coma. I told her my flight was scheduled to leave Manila on Sunday because I needed to return to my job and my son, who was staying with his kindergarten teacher. I was inside the U.S. embassy, but I didn't have anyone to call, and I couldn't stay in the Philippines any longer than when I had left.

The cashier insisted that I needed to pay $1,600.00, and if I didn't, they couldn't stamp the visas for my boys. She suggested I use my credit card, but it was already full. I didn't want to get out of line because I knew I couldn't change plans or cancel the plane tickets. I couldn't call my family, and they didn't even know we were at the embassy because my kids were still under court-ordered protection from them.

I said to the cashier, "Can you excuse me? I'm going to the toilet. My sons will stand in the line." So, I went to the bathroom, closed the stall door, closed the lid of the toilet, kneeled, and began to pray. I sent a direct *telegram* to God in the bathroom of the U.S. Embassy. I prayed, "Lord, I know You have never abandoned us. I'm here with no money in my bank accounts. I need to pay again for my kids' visas. Lord, give me miracles again. I cannot leave the U.S. embassy, and I don't have the money in my account. I pray, Lord, show me what to do. I claim this promise in the Bible's text.

Jeremiah 33:3 says," Call unto me, and I will answer you and show you great and mighty things, which you know not."

Mark 9:23 says, "Jesus said to him, 'If you can believe, all things are possible to him that believes.'"

And I went back to the line, and the cashier suggested I try my ATM card. I agreed, but in my mind, I knew I only had five hundred dollars in my account. I needed to pay for parking my car at the airport in Los Angeles upon my return. But I had faith, and I believed God would perform a miracle for us one more time. I gave my ATM card to the cashier, and I just trusted God. When the cashier said, "Approved," I thanked God. The bank had approved it but charged an overdraft fee. I said, "Lord, it's okay."

Then, the cashier gave me the receipt, and she told me to go to the next window for the passport. So, I went to that window, and I was waiting for my boy's passports. The person asked me to get him the address of where I was staying in Manila so they could deliver the passports there. I said we were staying in the hotel near the embassy, but we would be checking out Sunday because our flight was scheduled to leave at 7:00 p.m.

The man told me the passport would be delivered next week. I said, "Sir, stamp my boys' visas and passports. I cannot cancel my flight, and I don't have any money to extend my stay. I need to return to my job. I have a six-year-old son who I left with a teacher. Please, Sir, we cannot wait until next week." But he said he could not help me because they needed to deliver the passport. So, I gave the address of my half-brother because we would only stay in the hotel until Sunday. I now only had three hundred dollars cash for our food and needs until our flight left on Sunday. I hoped for the best, but I was disappointed again with all the trials I faced.

I was crying, but I didn't want to show my three boys because they had just recovered from the trauma of their abuse and had been released from the hospital. I felt as if I had experienced nothing but trials and disappointment. I was so down and weak. But I wanted to show my kids that we wouldn't give up, so I was still smiling at them. I called my half-brother and asked him to please pick us up at the embassy.

He was a couple of years older than me, and we had never met, so he was surprised when I called. I said, "Please don't tell anyone we are here, even the father of my boys. Can we stay in your home just to wait for my boys' passports? I'm worried because our flight is on Sunday, and today is Friday. I can't stay longer than Sunday." My brother's home was small, but I said to him, "Even if we just sit down on the couch, we are okay."

That night, I was crying in the bathroom. I said to God, "Why? All these problems are too much to bear." I wouldn't be able to extend the plane tickets. I was staying with my brother, who I didn't know, and I had only three hundred dollars in my wallet. Again, I cried to God and claimed the same promise in the Bible. I said, "Lord, show me another miracle so we can fly on Sunday. How can I bring my sons if I don't have their passports?"

Later that night, my three boys all slept in my lap on the couch. I cried again before falling asleep. I woke up Saturday morning and said to the boys, "Let's go to the church." I asked my brother where the church was located, so we rode a tricycle there as it was ten minutes from his house. I thanked God in advance for all the blessings. And as for the trials I was experiencing, I gave everything to God.

We stayed with my brother Saturday night. I was praying and waiting for God to perform miracles for us. That night, I went to the bathroom, and I turned on the shower faucet. I was crying loudly to God because my trials were too much to bear. I just surrendered everything in our lives to God. That night, we all slept on the couch again; my sons were leaning on me the whole night.

Early the following day, Sunday, November 5th, 2005, at 6:00 a.m., Someone I was knocking on the door. THE MAN was riding a motorcycle and asked for me by my name. I said yes, it was me. He had a package for me, and I was jumping for joy because I knew God had answered my prayers. The person from the U.S. Embassy delivered my three boys' passports. I hugged the man, and I said, "Thanks, God. You sent us angels so we can fly tonight, and we don't need to change our tickets. We can go back to the USA as planned, to my youngest son and my job."

We serve a God of the impossible. God answered my prayers so many times in unexpected and unimaginable ways. Our God is awesome. I cannot thank He was enough for my life; He sent me so many angels to save my kids and me.

When we were on the airplane, I was so excited to have my boys with me. We flew from the Philippines to Los Angeles and arrived safely. I did not sleep much on the airplane because I was overjoyed that God was showing me multiple miracles when I was bringing my three sons to the USA. When we arrived in Los Angeles, I was so excited to have my boys with me that I took them directly to the school so they could meet their brother, my youngest son. We were overjoyed and gave thanks to God.

I quickly went to the bank to address the use of my ATM card at the embassy in Manila when I had to pay for the visas. I asked them how much I had an overdraft, but the bank teller said I didn't overdraft at all. I told her that wasn't possible and that I had the receipt from that Friday, November 3rd, 2005. I asked her to check the date, and she said on that day, someone deposited cash into my account. The person who made the deposit didn't give their name but just provided my name and account number. I said to the bank teller, "Thank you so much." I knew it was God's angel who deposited money into my account that day. I praise God for His mercy, love, and goodness. This is my life, and I cannot thank God enough.

Positive Affirmations to Believe in Yourself and What's Possible
- "Believe in yourself and all that you are. Know that there is something inside you that is greater than any obstacle."

  – Christian D.
- "Desire backed by faith knows no such word as impossible."

  -Napoleon Hill
- "Action is the real measure of intelligence."

  -Napoleon Hill
- "All thoughts which have been emotionalized (given feeling) and mixed with faith (expectancy), begin immediately to translate themselves into their physical equivalent."
- "You become what you think about."
- "You give mefore you get."
- "You can do it if you believe you can."

-Napoleon Hill

Bible Verses that Inspired My Everyday Thanksgiving Over Joyful Miracles

1 Chronicles 16:34

"Give thanks to the Lord, for he is good; his love endures forever."

Colossians 3:15-17 ESV

"And let the peace of Christ rule in your hearts, to which indeed you were called in one body. And be thankful. Let the word of Christ dwell in you richly, teaching and admonishing one another in all wisdom, singing psalms and hymns and spiritual songs, with thankfulness in your hearts to God. And whatever you do, in word or deed, do everything in the name of the Lord Jesus, giving thanks to God the Father through him."

Philippians 4:6 ESV

"Do not be anxious about anything, but in everything by Prayer and supplication with thanksgiving let your requests be made known to God."

Psalm 30:12 ESV

"That my glory may sing your praise and not be silent. O Lord my God, I will give thanks to you forever!"

Isaiah 12:4-5 ESV

"And you will say in that day: 'Give thanks to the Lord, call upon his name, make known his deeds among the peoples, proclaim that his name is exalted. Sing praises to the Lord, for he has done gloriously; let this be made known in all the earth.'"

Hebrews 12:28-29 NASB1995

"Therefore, since we receive a kingdom which cannot be shaken, let us show gratitude, by which we may offer to God an acceptable service with reverence and awe, for our God, is a consuming fire."

Jonah 2:9 NASB1995

"But I will sacrifice to You with the voice of thanksgiving. That which I have vowed I will pay. Salvation is from the Lord."

1 Timothy 4:4-5 NASB1995

"For everything created by God is good, and nothing is to be rejected, if it is received with gratitude, for it is sanctified by means of the word of God and Prayer."

Chapter 23
Forgiveness Is the Best Revenge

When I started living in the USA in 1994, I was suffering from the pain of the past. Every day since I was five years old, I remember being abused and struggling. It followed me from my childhood and into my marriage. It was terrible at the time, but I was praying to God to help me forget and forgive those who abused me, my family, and my husband.

One day, I received a letter from my auntie, who had almost killed me when she tied me to the coconut tree for eight hours and hit me with a very sharp stick that cut my skin and made me bleed until I was almost near death. I had been punished for my other relatives' mistakes. When I read the letter from her, I cried because this was the incident I remembered.

In her letter, she asked me to forgive her. She said she was sick and asked me to help her and forgive her. She told me she needed medication every day for her diabetes and for a stroke. I knelt after reading the letter and asked God to help me have forgiveness. Her letter melted my heart, and I sent her money until she died eleven years later. I was supporting her needs because she wasn't married and had no children. It was a relief in my heart for the hurt I had carried for however many years when I was growing up.

When my ex-husband abused me too much and almost killed me, it was tough because I was suffering to take care of four boys alone. He never helped me, even when they were small. And, the other family, who rejected me and abandoned me, I let it all go. You see, my best revenge was forgiveness, and I helped all of them, even if I was struggling to survive in the USA and to support and raise my four boys alone.

I was suffering from all those traumatic moments in my life, and my children suffered too much as well. When my ex-husband and my sister abused my kids and caused my Son to be in a coma for two months, I struggled to pay the hospital bills. I was loaded with debt just to save my son's life. I carried everything alone with no help from my family or their Father. When my kids came to the USA, I still had trouble supporting them. We were homeless because I couldn't afford to pay all the debts I had incurred. It was so hard to be a single mother to four sons at twenty-seven years old.

But every time I gave up, I would dream. God showed me in my dreams the stories in the Bible about Joseph, about Job, about the widow lady, and other stories in the Bible. It was tough to forgive the cruelty and trauma both my boys and I had experienced in my life. We were struggling just for our daily needs, and it was so overwhelming to deal with these problems.

When God changed my heart to let everything go and move forward, I forgave everyone who caused my pain and my children's pain. We had already suffered too much. I prayed to God to give me a forgiving heart towards those who had done wrong to me. My best revenge was to forgive them, love them all, and help them because God gave me a new heart to forgive all and let it go.

The article "Forgiveness Affirmations" gives you "some affirmations to help wash away the pain of resentment to a more loving, fresher, cleaner and joyful life."

- "I am free from the prison of resentment."
- "Resentment replicated old turmoil, and I chose my life to be drama free."
- "Forgiveness is a gift to myself."
- "When I forgive myself, it becomes easier to forgive others."
- "Forgiveness gives me a fresh start and a clean slate."[14]

Bible Verses About Forgiveness

Colossians 3:13

"Bear with each other and forgive one another if any of you has a grievance against someone. Forgive as the Lord forgave you."

Matthew 6:14-15

"For if you forgive other people when they sin against you, your heavenly Father will also forgive you. But if you do not forgive others their sins, your Father will not forgive your sins."

Luke 17:3-4

---

[14] Gerald Crawford, "Forgiveness Affirmations," A Course in Forgiveness, August 27, 2020, https://acourseinforgiveness.co.za/forgiveness-affirmations.

"So, watch yourselves. 'If your brother or sister sins against you, rebuke them; and if they repent, forgive them. 4 Even if they sin against you, seven times in a day, and seven times come back to you saying, 'I repent,' you must forgive them.'"

Ephesians 4:31-32

"Get rid of all bitterness, rage and anger, brawling and slander, along with every form of malice. Be kind and compassionate to one another, forgiving each other, just as in Christ God forgave you."

1 John 1:9

"If we confess our sins, he is faithful and just and will forgive us our sins and purify us from all unrighteousness."

Isaiah 43:25-26

"I, even I, am he who blots out your transgressions, for my own sake, and remembers your sins no more. Review the past for me. Let us argue the matter together; state the case for your innocence."

Acts 3:19

"Repent, then, and turn to God, so that your sins may be wiped out, that times of refreshing may come from the Lord."

Isaiah 1:18

"'Come now, let us settle the matter,' says the LORD. 'Though your sins are like scarlet, they shall be as white as snow, though they are red as crimson, they shall be like wool.'"

2 Corinthians 5:17

"Therefore, if anyone is in Christ, the new creation has come: The old has gone, the news is here!"

Ephesians 1:7

"In him, we have redemption through his blood, the forgiveness of sins, in accordance with the riches of God's grace."

Hebrews 10:17

"Then he adds: 'Their sins and lawless acts I will remember no more.'"

Daniel 9:9

"The Lord our God is merciful and forgiving, even though we have rebelled against him."

Colossians 1:13-14

"For he has rescued us from the dominion of darkness and brought us into the kingdom of the Son he loves, in whom we have redemption, the forgiveness of sins."

Psalm 103:12

"As far as the east is from the west, so far has he removed our transgressions from us."

Numbers 14:19-21

"'In accordance with your great love, forgive the sin of these people, just as you have pardoned them from the time they left Egypt until now.' The LORD replied, 'I have forgiven them, as you asked. Nevertheless, as surely as I live and as surely as the glory of the LORD fills the whole earth.'"

Micah 7:18-19

"Who is a God like you, who pardons sin and forgives the transgression of the remnant of his inheritance? You do not stay angry forever but delight in showing mercy. You will again have compassion on us; you will tread our sins underfoot and hurl all our iniquities into the depths of the sea."

Matthew 6:9-15

"This, then, is how you should pray: 'Our Father in heaven, hallowed be your name, your kingdom come, you will be done, on earth as it is in heaven. Give us today our daily bread. And forgive us our debts, as we also have forgiven our debtors. And lead us not into temptation, but deliver us from the evil one.' For if you forgive other people when they sin against you, your heavenly Father will also forgive you. But if you do not forgive others their sins, your Father will not forgive your sins."

Mark 11:25

"And when you stand praying, if you hold anything against anyone, forgive them, so that your Father in heaven may forgive you your sins."

Chapter 24
Angel Miracle

My boys had been in the USA only one week when another issue struck us. On the second week of November in 2005, I was in a bad accident. I went to work at the home of my private patient in Venice Beach, California. I was parking my car in the parking lot near their house, and I saw the couple's handicapped van parked in their driveway. I saw the husband unloading the electric wheelchair from the back of the car while the wife was trying to sit down in her manual wheelchair, but it began to roll down the driveway.

When I saw the wheelchair start to roll, I ran towards the old lady to catch her and stop her from falling on the ground. I caught and stabilized her, then retrieved the wheelchair. After placing the woman in her wheelchair, I adjusted the footrests so she could put her feet on them. She had Parkinson's and shook severely. While on my knees helping her get settled in the manual wheelchair, the husband unloaded the electric wheelchair but wasn't paying attention to his surroundings. As he unloaded the electric chair from the car ramp, he forgot to lock the ramp, and it began to move toward the ground. I helped the elderly woman. I was close to the car ramp with the wheelchair still on it. As the ramp dropped to the ground, the electric wheelchair ran into me and hit me in the chest. I heard my ribs crack, and it became difficult to breathe.

At the time, I still managed to stand up and drive myself to Glendale to see my doctor. At the doctor's office, I was x-rayed right away. I had five cracked ribs, and they were pushing into my lungs. Hence, the doctor ordered an ambulance to take me to Olive View Hospital. Still, all the ambulances were busy, so I asked my friend to drive me to the hospital. The hospital doctor told me they couldn't help me because by the time I reached the hospital, my ribs had punctured my lungs, and my lungs had collapsed. There was no way to do surgery, and I was going to die. I was in excruciating pain and dying. For the pain, the doctor ordered morphine. Everything else in my body was fine except for my broken ribs and collapsed lungs. The nurses shot the morphine close to my heart because the hospital staff didn't think I would live. The morphine was administered to ease my pain, as they thought I was dying. I didn't die, and I was moved to the ICU. The doctor had given up on me, but I had not given up on myself and still believed I would survive. I cried during the entire hospital stay. I knew I wasn't dying.

I was worried about my four boys. They were all still young—fourteen, thirteen, twelve, and seven years old. The doctor called the school and told them about my accident and that I was in the hospital. The school told my boys they were worried about me. My second Son went to all the teachers asking for prayers for me and asked all the churches in Glendale to pray for me. Nobody was watching my kids full-time; the teachers were all helping the boys by providing them with food, dropping them off at school, and taking them home. I thanked God for all the teachers at the Glendale Adventist Academy in Glendale, California. I didn't want my kids to see me in the hospital hooked up to machinery, so I would not let them come visit me. They had all been in the hospital in the Philippines due to the abuse they experienced. I didn't want any bad memories to flood their mind by seeing me in the hospital. I was praying to God to just let me live until my boys graduated from college.

I was praying to God to give me a miracle. In my mind, I said to God, *I passed death so many times in my life. I'm going to live. I still believe, God, you will show me a miracle like when You woke my oldest Son, after two months of being comatose.* I prayed because nothing is impossible, and I believed it. I was crying because even the doctor had given up on me.

I began singing songs in my mind that had given me courage through all my trials since I was a child. I was singing them in my hospital bed because, in my mind, I believed I was going to survive and not die. The first song I sang was "He Touched Me." The chorus of this song says, "He touched me, oh, He felt me. And oh, the joy that floods my soul. Something happened, and now I know He touched me and made me whole."[15] My second favorite song to sing was "Lily of the Valley" By Charles W. Fry (1881):

I've found a friend in Jesus. He's everything to me,

---

[15] William J Gaither, "He Touched Me," Nashville: RCA Studio B, February 29, 1972.

He's the fairest of ten thousand to my soul;

The Lily of the Valley, in Him alone, I see

All I need is to cleanse and make myself entirely whole.

In sorrow, He's my comfort; in trouble, He's my stay;

He tells me every care on Him to roll.

Refrain:

He's the Lily of the Valley, the Bright and Morning Star,

He's the fairest of ten thousand to my soul.

He all my grief has taken, and all my sorrows borne;

In temptation, He's my strong and mighty tower;

I've all for Him forsaken, and all my idols torn.

From my heart, and now He keeps me by His power.

Though all the world forsakes me, and Satan tempts me sore,

Through Jesus, I shall safely reach the goal.

He'll never, never leave me, nor yet forsake me here,

While I live by faith and do His blessed will,

A wall of fire about me, I've nothing now to fear,

From His manna, He, my hungry soul shall fill.

Then, sweeping up to glory to see His blessed face,

Where rivers of delight shall ever roll.

    I kept singing these songs as I was lying in my hospital bed in the ICU.

After four weeks of being in the ICU, my kidneys began shutting down, and my body was retaining too much water from the IV drip. The only medicine they were giving me was antibiotics and morphine. Eight weeks passed in the ICU, and my heart was still pumping, and I was still talking to all the doctors and nurses. But shortly after that, I started losing my voice, and I could only write on a notepad to the nurse and doctor to communicate. My mind was still alert, and I was still making decisions for everything.

On Friday, I had an allergic reaction to the medication, and my face and body began to itch. At that point, the doctor told me they only gave me twenty-four hours to live. That same day, around 6:00 p.m., when all the doctors had given up on me, they told me they would remove my life support that night. The hospital social worker told me I needed to sign a Do Not Resuscitate (DNR) document and place my kids up for adoption.

I was told that the doctors would take me off the support at 7:00 p.m. After I had signed the documents. Since I had a difficult time talking to the hospital staff for the past four weeks, it was tough to explain that even though my body was shutting down, my mind was still listening and alert. By this time, even my muscles were losing strength, and I could barely write on the notepad by my bed. I listened to the doctors' and nurses' advice about my medical condition and their thoughts about my life. Since I could barely talk or even write my thoughts on the notepad, I was helpless. Most of my body was in pain. My prayers to God were to give me extra life.

I said to God, "You have saved me many times in my life when I was a child and as I grew up. Now I believe and know that I'm going to survive."

The doctors were so sure I was dying because my kidneys were shutting down, and they could not give me any more morphine because they were failing. The hospital staff had all given up hope and wanted to remove my life support so I could die peacefully. At 6:30 p.m., I was telling the doctor I believed I wasn't dying, but they thought otherwise. I had already signed the DNR and adoption papers and realized I didn't have any choice other than the hospital staff removing my life support. So, I asked, "Can I have three wishes because I am dying?"

My three wishes were:

1. First, I said, "I belong to SDA church. I am a member of the Southern California conference. Can you call a pastor to pray for me before I die?"
2. My second wish was to see my four boys alone, and I asked for someone from church to bring them to the hospital after service.
3. Finally, I wrote down a recipe for my kidneys because I needed to save them. I asked the nurse on duty for this to be my third wish. I asked her to please do me a huge favor and make this raw juice for me and bring it to the hospital because it would save my kidneys. The nurse asked the

doctor if I could have the juice, and he said to give me anything I wanted because I was dying anyway.

So, the nurse called her husband in the late afternoon, and he did as his wife asked. The man went to the market, bought the ingredients, then went home and made the juice following the recipe I said to the nurse. The man brought the juice to the hospital after work at about 9:00 p.m. on Friday. The nurse also called the church office to have a pastor come pray for me. The pastor would pray with me the following day, Saturday, at 10:00 a.m. Some teachers from my children's school agreed to bring my boys to visit me on Saturday at noon. I was happy because all my wishes were done.

Around 6:45 p.m., the nurse was keeping watch over me through the window to my room in the ICU. She would come into the room to wipe my tears and swab my dry mouth because they had already stopped the IV fluids. The nurse was waiting to remove my life support in fifteen minutes at 7:00 p.m. The nurse couldn't leave me because I was in critical condition, so she watched me through the ICU window or sat by my bedside.

I'm not sure how or why, but the next thing I know, I was alone in the room, and someone wearing all white clothes, with his face so bright—like sunshine — came to my bed. He picked up a tissue and wiped my tears. He put the tissue on the table and then held my right hand. His other hand touched my head and my shoulders and then grabbed my left hand. He said to me, "I will pray for you."

I said, "Please, pray for me."

And then, after the prayer, he picked up the tissue and wiped away my tears again. He touched the top of my head and my shoulders and felt my left hand for a second time. As he left the room heading towards the door, I opened my eyes, but His face was so bright I couldn't see his face. I said, "Thank you, God, for sending an angel to touch me and pray for me." I knew God had answered my prayers and sent another angel with a miracle. I knew I was not dying.

I didn't know it at the time, but when the nurse came into the room, she saw the notepad with words written on it. She knew I hadn't written it because I had lost all strength in my arm and hand, so I was unable to write, but I knew the angel had written me a message. He wrote two things to me on my notepad:

1. Go home to your kids.
2. Make a difference.

Then he shut the door.

The Angel of the Lord also wrote the following Bible verse on my notepad:

"Teaching them to observe all things whatsoever I have commanded you: And lo, I am with you always, even unto the end of the world. Amen." -Matthew 28:20 (KJV)

That Inspired Me

In her book, *Step to Christ*, Ellen G. Whit says, "God never asks us to believe without giving sufficient evidence upon which to base our faith. His existence, His character, and the truthfulness of His word are all established by testimony that appeals to our reason, and this testimony is abundant. Yet God has never removed the possibility of doubt. Our faith must rest upon evidence, not demonstration. Those who wish to doubt will have the opportunity, while those who desire to know the truth will find plenty of evidence on which to rest their faith."[16]

Bible Verses That Inspired Me

Matthew 19:26 KJV

"With men, this is impossible, but with God, all things are possible."

Philippians 4:13 NKJV

"I can do all things through Christ who strengthens me."

Psalm 31:14 NKJV

"I trust in you, O Lord; I say, 'You are my God.'"

Hebrews 11:1

"Now faith is confidence in what we hope for and assurance about what we do not see."

2 Corinthians 5:7

---

[16] Ellen G. White, *Step to Christ* (Idaho: Pacific Press Publishing Association, 2000), 105.

"For we live by faith, not by sight."

Romans 15:13

"May the God of hope fill you with all joy and peace as you trust in him so that you may overflow with hope by the power of the Holy Spirit."

Chapter 25

Impossible to Possible

Then God said, "I give you every seed-bearing plant on the face of the whole earth and every tree that has fruit with seed in it. They will be yours for food. -Genesis 1:29

When the door shut, my heart started beating harder. The nurse came back inside, and I asked the nurse, "Who was my visitor just now? He just left." I could suddenly speak again after the shining man had touched me.

And the nurse said, "No one came in."

I said, "No, just now, he prayed for me, and he was wearing white.

She said, "I was watching the door. No one came. I was waiting for fifteen minutes to remove your life support."

When the nurse said no, I thanked God because I knew it was an angel, and I knew I was going to live. I was not dying. He prayed for me. The nurse looked at the notepad next to my bed and saw that the writing there was not mine, and she said, "Wow, you will survive."

I said, "Yes, I believe I'm not dying because I know I'm going to live. I am just waiting for your husband to come with the juice. Just give it to me in the dropper slowly until I finish."

At 7:00 p.m., the nurse removed my life support. She watched me. I was crying, but in my mind, I was still singing "He Touched

Me" and "The Lily of the Valley." I also recalled my favorite texts in the Bible, Jeremiah 33:3, "Call to me, and I will answer you and show you great and mighty things, which you do not know" (NKJV); Jeremiah 33:6, "Behold, I will bring it health and cure, and I will cure them and will reveal to them the abundance of peace and truth" (KJV); Mark 9:23, "Jesus said to him, 'If you can believe, all things are possible to him who believes" (NKJV).

The nurse's husband arrived at 9:00 p.m. to bring my requested raw juice for my kidneys. The nurse gave the drops to me slowly until I finished the juice. She was crying, looking at me with sympathy because I was dying, leaving my four children with no father around. I said to her, "God sent me an Angel Miracle. I believe I'm going to survive and go home to my kids. And I will make a difference like the message he gave me."

The nurse patiently gave me the juice through the night from 9:00 and into the early morning. I finished the sixteen ounces of juice around 5:30 a.m., I peed a lot, and she noticed my heartbeat started getting better. The doctor came to my room and noticed I had peed. He ordered new blood tests and he discovered my kidneys had started to function again. The doctor was shocked, and he believed the juice helped me, and it was a miracle. The nurse was happy. Because my kidneys started to function again, the doctor and nurse put me back on life support.

I praised God, who had answered my prayers many times. I asked the doctor if I could continue to drink the juice, and he said,

"Yes, go ahead." He was surprised by how it worked and asked me how I knew the recipe, so I told him that God gave me a vision. I knew God wanted me to live so I could take care of my young children.

I was moved out of the ICU and into a regular room. The doctor could no longer give me any pain medication because of my kidneys, and he could only give me one antibiotic. When I was home after more than two months of being in the hospital, I continued to drink my own recipe to build my strength back up and help my bones heal. I was only drinking raw juice that I blended every day from vegetables, fruits, seeds, and nuts. I did this until my ribs healed, but my lung was still collapsed, and it would take a couple of years for it to return to normal. It was hard for me to breathe. I had plenty of fluids, but I drank different versions of my recipe. This was the recipe I had been using since 1994. I even gave the simple food one to my kids for their lunch box every day.

I praise God for everything, for the extra time in my life and for the Angel Miracle. I was on my deathbed, but I was always imagining that I was going to live. In my mind, I kept believing in the promises of God's words. I never gave up despite my pain or struggles because I trusted that God was and is the only Healer. The doctor was dressing my wounds, but God is the Healer.

And this is why I have shared my recipes through my company in the following forms:

- Miracle Mix
- Miracle Shake
- Miracle Mix Meal

These products are made only from natural foods like vegetables, fruits, nuts, seeds, and herbs. This is the original diet from God. He made the vegetables and fruits and the seeds and herbs for our healthy life.

Healing Bible Verses

Proverbs 4:20-22

"My Son, pay attention to what I say; turn your ear to my words. Do not let them out of your sight. Keep them within your heart, for they are life to those who find them and Health to one's whole body."

Psalm 107:19-21

"Then they cried to the LORD in their trouble, and he saved them from their distress. He sent forth his word and healed them; he rescued them from the grave. Let them give thanks to the LORD for his unfailing love and his wonderful deeds for mankind."

Jeremiah 17:14

"Heal me, LORD, and I will be healed; save me, and I will be saved, for you are the one I praise."

Mark 5:34

"He said to her, 'Daughter, your faith has healed you. Go in peace, and be freed from your suffering.'"

James 5:16

"Therefore, confess your sins to each other and pray for each other so that you may be healed. The prayer of a righteous person is powerful and effective."

Romans 8:38-39

"For I am convinced that neither death nor life, neither angels nor demons, neither the present nor the future, nor any powers, neither height nor depth nor anything else in all creation, will be able to separate us from the love of God that is in Christ Jesus our Lord."

Chapter 26
A Surprise Gift from God

My life continued to be challenging because of my collapsed lung following the accident. I was only working part-time, and my kids were in college and high school. It was tough to support our daily needs. I could not find a job full-time because my lung was still collapsed. We were struggling to pay our bills because I lost my home healthcare business. I started a private care agency for home caregivers, and it went bankrupt. It was so hard to be a single parent of four boys when I was still sick from the accident. At one point, I was three months behind on the rent for the house, all the utility bills, and credit card bills. I was stressed because of our situation. I had nothing to turn to but God.

It was a Friday when the electricity was cut off, and the landlord gave us notice that we needed to get out of the house. We were being evicted. We didn't have a place to go, and none of the shelters wanted to accept us because there were five of us. The boys and I packed as much of our belongings as we could, and we gave away everything else that was in the five-bedroom house. We left the house with a few clothes, our sleeping bags, and a tent. That afternoon, I called the church we attended and asked the pastor to pray for me and my situation because we had just become homeless.

The pastor said he was out of town and directed me to the elder of the church. When the boys arrived home from the SDA academy that afternoon, I told my boys we won't give up and we will never be discouraged. We knelt to pray to God and surrender everything to Him. I fell asleep that night around 7:00 p.m. It was the last night in the house. I dreamt about the story of the prophet Elijah and the widow lady in the Bible. As the dream was coming to an end, I woke up because my phone was ringing. The elder of the church said he would see us tomorrow in the church. I said, "Please, pray for us with anonymous prayers."

And after the call, I went back to sleep. Saturday morning, my boys and I went to church. There was a visiting pastor that Sabbath day who preached a sermon titled "Never Give Up." I was surprised because that was the same message from my dream the night before.

The elder of the church asked me to talk with him after church. When we spoke, he handed me an envelope with money in it. Inside was twelve thousand dollars cash, enough money for one year of living allowances. He also gave me the receipt for the payment of four months' back rent that was owed to the landlord. He paid the outstanding debt with his own money. He told me to find a two-bedroom apartment, and he would pay the rent for a year until my kids were finished at the SDA academy. I was shocked and surprised at how God had answered my prayers. We hung onto God's promises and God provided for me like he did for Elijah and the widow. God is the Father of the Fatherless. On that day, I knew God would never stop abandoning us no matter what we would go through. God was still in control, and we only needed to step out on faith in God and believe in His promise.

I know God is in my life, come whatever. No matter my troubles, concerns, or trials, God was still standing beside us. If we have faith and believe with a humble heart, He will hear us. "For the jar of flour was not used up and the jug of oil did not run dry, in keeping with the word of the LORD spoken by Elijah" (1 Kings 17:16). Elijah was as human as we are, and yet when he prayed earnestly that no rain would fall, none fell for three and a half years! Then, when he prayed again, the sky sent down rain, and the earth began to yield its crops (James 5:17-18).

Bible Verses About Never Giving Up

Psalm 31:24 ESV

"Be strong, and let your heart take courage. All of you who wait for the Lord!"

Philippians 4:12-13 ESV

"I know how to be brought low, and I know how to abound. In any and every circumstance, I have learned the secret of facing plenty and hunger, abundance and need. I can do all things through him who strengthens me."

Galatians 6:9 ESV

"And let us not grow weary of doing good, for in due season we will reap if we do not give up."

Romans 12:12 ESV

"Rejoice in hope, be patient in tribulation, be constant in prayer."

1 Corinthians 13:7 ESV

"Love bears all things, believes all things, hopes all things, endures all things."

Ephesians 4:26-24 ESV

"Be angry and do not sin; do not let the sun go down on your anger and give no opportunity to the devil. Let the thief no longer steal, but rather let him labor, doing honest work with his own hands, so that he may have something to share with anyone in need. Let no corrupting talk come out of your mouths, but only such as is good for building up, as fits the occasion, that it may give grace to those who hear. And do not grieve the Holy Spirit of God, by whom you were sealed for the day of redemption."

Joshua 1:9 ESV

"Have I not commanded you? Be strong and courageous. Do not be frightened, and do not be dismayed, for the Lord your God is with you wherever you go."

Philippians 1:6 ESV

"And I am sure of this, that he who began a good work in you will bring it to completion on the day of Jesus Christ."

Isaiah 41:10 ESV

"Fear not, for I am with you; be not dismayed, for I am your God; I will strengthen you, I will help you, I will uphold you with my righteous right hand."

Matthew 11:28-30 ESV

"Come to me, all who labor and are heavily laden, and I will give you rest. Take my yoke upon you, and learn from me, for I am gentle and lowly in heart, and you will find rest for your souls. For my yoke is easy, and my burden is light."

Psalm 71:14 ESV

"But I will hope continually and will praise you yet more and more."

Romans 12:19 ESV

"Beloved, never revenge yourselves, but leave it to the wrath of God, for it is written, 'Vengeance is mine, I will repay,' says the Lord."

Chapter 27
Miracles from an Angel on a Motorcycle and Tsunami Yolanda

I was so busy working two jobs to support my four boys as a single mom. I needed to be sure my boys were cared for, so I rented rooms in my house to nurses or caregivers, with the understanding that they needed to help me manage my kids while I worked. As I worked during this time, I kept dreaming of a place I had never seen or visited before. I had the dream repeatedly. It turns out the location was the island in Tacloban City, Leyte, Philippines.

Over time, I had multiple dreams about three schools. First, I saw the schools and then the name of each of them, one of which was Kanmarating, Leyte, Philippines Elementary School. Then I saw the kids sitting on the floor because they had no chairs. The other two schools had a few chairs, so some of the children sat on the dirt floor. The first school had 250 students, the second school had 100 to 150 students, and the third school had more than 200 students. Each village had a school, and between the three villages, the schools had almost 650 students. These villages were impoverished and located in the mountains of Kanmarating, Leyte, Philippines. The name of the principal teacher was highlighted in my dream. I kept ignoring the dream, but after a few times having it, I researched the name of the school and the address. I wrote it down and kept the paper hidden.

One day, I prayed to God. I asked, "Why am I dreaming about this place? I'm so busy in the U.S." I worked, cared for my kids, and saved the extra money. I didn't put the money in the bank; I kept the cash and saved it. I had saved a few thousand dollars and checked to see if I could fly to visit the place, but the problem was I didn't know anyone there. I asked a friend on Facebook if he knew of the place I researched. He did, and when I asked him if it was safe to visit, he said, "Yes." So, I decided to make the trip.

I prayed to visit the location, and I booked tickets and hotels in Tacloban City, Leyte, but I needed to rent a car to go to the village school, which was three hours away from the city in the mountains. I just kept praying God would watch over me. I visited the place, and the school I saw in my dream was exactly the same in real life. The kids were sitting on the floor in school. I went to the three schools and talked to the principal who oversaw the three schools, but I have yet to tell them I was from the USA. I just said I was from Manila.

I visited each of the three schools to see if what I dreamt about the village was real. I told the principal I would come back, as I stayed for a one-week vacation from my Job and then would head back to the USA. On the last day of my visit to the hotel in Tacloban City, someone knocked on my room door at 5:00a.m. It was a man on a motorcycle, and he asked me, "Can you help a lady who is very sick? She is my friend's wife. She is two hours away." He told me she was bleeding very badly. I didn't know the motorcyclist, but he knew the taxi driver who drove me to the small town that was in my dream and that I had visited.

I asked him, "Why me? I'm not a doctor."

The man pleaded, "Just go with me. I will take you there."

I told him she needed to go to the hospital. He explained she had already been to the hospital. They sent her away because they didn't have enough money, so her husband brought her home to the mountain village. After hearing this, I said OKAY.

Before we left, I told him, "Just wait outside." Then I prayed, "Lord, I don't know this person. Just protect me. I trust you, God. I believe You will be with me and protect me."

Then, I went to join the man on the motorcycle. I brought only my small bag with my Bible and my passport. We traveled to the mountain, and when we were on the top of the mountain, we drove on a rugged road that only a single motorcycle could drive on. When I got to the house, I could tell they were inferior. They lived in a Nipa Hut made of bamboo. The husband was trying to comfort his wife. She was young, only twenty years old. Before doing anything, I prayed to the Lord to help us with what to do. She was bleeding, but I didn't know what I should do and didn't have any medicine. Then, I saw that their backyard was full of vegetables, coconuts, and bananas.

I said to the husband, "Get the water from a coconut and bring it to me." I got some cayenne peppers from the backyard, and I began smashing them until I got the juice of the peppers. I added this to the coconut water, and I then gave it to the lady by spoon. I said, "Keep drinking because we don't have medicine. Only God can hear our prayers." I prayed to God to give us a miracle again. I claimed the promises of God in the Bible. "LORD my God, I called to you for help, and you healed me" (Ps. 30:2). "Come to me, all you who are weary and burdened, and I will give you rest" (Matt. 11:28). The only medicine I brought were the promises of God and belief and faith in God.

After one hour, the blood was subsiding and slowly began to stop. When I had been there for three hours, I said to the husband, "Can you call the man who drove me here on the motorcycle?" I wanted to go back to the hotel because the sky was starting to get gloomy, and there was a strong wind. It looked like there would be a storm.

The husband said, "I don't know the man who brought you to my home this morning."

"Really?" I asked.

The husband said, "Yes, I don't know him. I never told anyone that I brought my wife home from the hospital because we don't have money."

I said, "He was an angel who brought me to your home." But then I asked the husband, "Can you find anyone to get me back to the hotel? I need a ride to go back, and it is getting darker now and starting to rain with strong winds." I was worried about how I would get back to the hotel because of my flight that day.

The husband said, "Okay, stay with my wife, and I will go down to look for someone to take you back to the hotel." But two hours passed, and he hadn't returned. The sky was getting darker, and the wind and rain were getting stronger. I started to get worried.

I prayed to God, "Please help me to make it back, and thank you, Lord, for healing the lady and stopping her bleeding."

When the husband returned, he told me, "I'm sorry. I cannot find anyone to take you back to the hotel, and the rain is getting heavy, and the wind is so strong." He continued, "Ma'am, there is a giant tsunami and a big storm. I heard from the captain of the village that the water had come up high and washed out the people's homes. The hotel was washed out, too. The only building standing is the Seventh Day Adventist church in Tacloban City."

"What?" I was shocked. I said, "Thank you, God. You sent me a single motorcycle angel to save my life by bringing me to the mountains to save me and help the lady who was bleeding."

I didn't have any choice but to stay in the house, so there were three of us in the small bamboo home. I just kept praying to God to save us because the wind was too strong, but the house was still standing. All the trees, the fruits, and the branches were broken and shattered on the ground, but the tiny house we were in was still standing. God was excellent, and He sent angels to watch us.

The tsunami, called Yolanda, destroyed Tacloban City. It was a massive storm that washed out houses and hotels. The luggage that I had left at the hotel was gone. Thousands of people died that day.

Even when the storm passed, I couldn't go back to the airport because the airport had been washed out by the storm, too. I was on the top of the mountain with this couple, and we didn't have any food or water. We could only eat the coconuts and drink the coconut juice.

I prayed to God, "Please send someone who can help us." We had no way to contact anyone, no cell phone, no power, nothing. I didn't have any extra clothes; all I had was my Bible and passport. I continued to pray, and the following day, I said, "God, I know You are with us." I memorized Psalm 91, Psalm 23, and Psalm 121.

Psalm 91 KJV

He that dwelleth in the secret place of the Highest shall abide under the shadow of the Almighty. I will say of the Lord, He is my refuge and my fortress: my God; in him will I trust. Surely, he shall deliver thee from the snare of the fowler and from the noisome pestilence. He shall cover thee with his feathers, and under his wings shalt thou trust: his truth shall be thy shield and buckler. Thou shalt not be afraid for the terror by night; nor for the arrow that fleet by day; Nor for the pestilence that walketh in darkness; nor for the destruction that wastes at noonday. A thousand shall fall at thy side, and ten thousand at thy right hand, but it shall not come nigh thee. Only with thine eyes shalt thou behold and see the reward of the wicked. Because thou hast made the Lord, which is my refuge, even the Highest, thy habitation; There shall no evil befall thee, neither shall any plague come nigh thy dwelling. For he shall give his angels charge over thee, to keep thee in all thy ways. They shall bear thee up in their hands, lest thou dash thy foot against a stone. Thou shalt tread upon the lion and adder: the young lion and the dragon shalt thou trample under feet. Because he hath set his love upon me, therefore, will I deliver him: I will set him on high because he hath known my name. He shall call upon me, and I will answer him: I will be with him in trouble; I will deliver him and honor him. With long life will I satisfy him, and shew him my salvation.

Psalm 23 KJV

The Lord is my shepherd; I shall not want. He makes me lie down in green pastures: he leadeth me beside the still waters. He restoreth my soul: he leadeth me in the paths of righteousness for his name's sake. Yea, though I walk through the valley of the shadow of death, I will fear no evil: for thou art with me; thy rod and thy staff they comfort me. Thou preparest a table before me in the presence of my enemies: thou anointers my head with oil; my cup runneth over. Surely goodness and mercy shall follow me all the days of my life: and I will dwell in the house of the Lord forever.

Psalm 121 KJV

I will lift up mine eyes unto the hills, from whence cometh my help. My help cometh from the Lord, which made heaven and earth. He will not suffer thy foot to be moved: he that keypath there will not slumber. Behold, he that keepeth Israel shall neither slumber nor sleep. The Lord is thy keeper: the Lord is thy shade upon thy right hand. The sun shall not smite thee by day, nor the moon by night.

The Lord shall preserve thee from all evil: he shall keep thy soul. The Lord shall keep thy going out and thy coming in from this time forth, and even for evermore.

After I memorized these chapters in the Bible, I was not worried anymore. I knew God would provide us our needs, then I started singing.

"A Shelter in the Time of Storm"
The Lord's our rock, in Him we hide,
A shelter in the time of storm;
Secure whatever I betide,
A shelter in the time of storm.
Mighty Rock in a weary land,
Cooling shade on the burning sand,
Faithful guide for the pilgrim band—
A shelter in the time of storm.
A shade by day, defense by night,
A shelter in the time of storm;
No fears alarm, no fears affright,
A shelter in the time of storm.
Mighty Rock in a weary land,
Cooling shade on the burning sand,
Faithful guide for the pilgrim band—
A shelter in the time of storm.

The raging storms may round us beat,
A shelter in the time of storm;
We'll never leave our safe retreat,
A shelter in the time of storm.
Mighty Rock in a weary land,
Cooling shade on the burning sand,
Faithful guide for the pilgrim band—
A shelter in the time of storm.
O Rock divine, O Refuge dear,
A Shelter in the time of storm;
He Thou our helper ever nearby,
A Shelter in the time of storm.
Mighty Rock in a weary land,
Cooling shade on the burning sand,
Faithful guide for the pilgrim band—
A shelter in the time of storm.[17]

After I sang, I heard a helicopter flying very low, near where we were located, and then I saw it was a Red Cross helicopter from the USA. I went outside and looked up to see the helicopter was very low, and it dropped boxes in front of the couple's home. We picked up the six boxes dropped, and they were filled with instant food, canned foods, towels, clothes, and personal hygiene products. It was

---

[17] Vernon J. Charlesworth, "A Shelter in the Time of Storm," (1880).

a miracle. God provided for our needs, and I stopped worrying about being taken care of after this event.

I was, however, worried about how I would get back to Manila. There was no airport and no way to communicate with anyone. I was on top of the mountain for two weeks with the couple, and we were lucky to survive when thousands of others had died. At this point, I saw a large cargo ship from the top of the mountain; the water level was so high it had brought the ship inland. But as the water receded, the ship was stuck in the mountainside.

I was worried that my kids didn't know if I was alive or not. Plus, no one knew where I was. It was a shocking experience, and I couldn't understand why incidents like this had been happening to me since childhood.

After two weeks, I managed to get back to Manila. I rode a cargo ship going to Manila because no flights were available. I needed to borrow money from my sister, who lived in Manila, so I could buy tickets to return to the USA. It was a very terrible experience for me. I saw lots of dead people in the streets caused by the flood; there were families and kids. Thousands of people died in that tsunami. I am so thankful to God that he saved my life and sent an angel on a motorcycle to take me to the top of the mountain to protect me and the couple. When I got back to the USA, I never told my kids or family details about what happened because I was shocked by the experience.

A year later, I returned to the school because I had been dreaming of giving away school supplies to thousands of families and kids and feeding them my healthy smoothies and Miracle Mix products. I made a couple of medical mission trips to, Tacloban City, Philippines. I praise God for everything. His promises are with me everywhere I go, and anytime we need Him, He is there. All I needed to do was step out in faith and believe it.

When I visited Tacloban City, Leyte, for the first time, I felt pity for those kids. They had no shoes on their feet and no chairs in the classrooms. I told the principal about the raw juice I made and that I wanted to teach their parents about eating healthy. I wanted to give the kids lunch, and I would go to the other two schools over the next two days. I spoke to the principal because all three schools shared the same one. A permit was needed before I helped the villages, so I asked if I could have permission to bring a captain, the highest-ranking official, to the Barangay village, and she said yes.

I didn't know anyone here, so I asked the teacher and my driver if they knew how I could get volunteers to help me. I told them I thought we could use ten young teenagers because I wanted to give the kids a free lunch at all three schools. Quickly, I had ten volunteers and a teacher to help me. This was the best moment in my life. It made me so happy to serve others because God had given me extra life after this tragedy and others. God saved my life so many times when I was a child, but it was apparent God was still with me. Now, I was devoting my life to making a difference for others.

Chapter 28
Surprise Trip to Australia

In 2016, I had a dream that I was in Australia, and I manufactured health food products. I dreamt that I studied healthy foods and that I wrote my story when I was there.

When I decided to make a change in my life, my kids were mad at me. They weren't talking to me. I decided to travel to Australia and to Asian countries to help others. I wanted to change my life story, but my kids didn't understand why I was traveling to volunteer for medical mission trips. I was so tired of my life, only working to support my kids and me. When they graduated college and could manage for themselves, I was so happy.

They didn't know my story of what I had been through since I was a child. They didn't know what I did to get myself and them out of our miserable lives in the Philippines. I did my best to save them and give them a new life in the USA. Now that they were grown, I was glad. I decided to use my life to serve others. My goal for this book is to inspire lots of people around the world when they see how God has been working in my life every day. I am totally dependent on God and no one else. I learned to have more confidence and courage to fight hardships and obstacles.

In 2017, I traveled to Australia to attend a business convention. I was not planning on attending the convention because I was so busy, but my business mentor, who was part of a multi-level marketing company that was hosting the meeting, wanted me to go. She was from Australia and encouraged me to attend the conference. She told me that I could buy a ticket and fly there the same day, but I needed an Australian visa, and that usually took twenty-four hours to receive by email. So, I prayed to God and said, "God, if it is Your will, you will show me a sign that I should go by getting the visa in less than twenty-four hours." I thought it would be too late, but it was God's will because I got the visa the same day I applied for it, and I was able to book the plane and convention tickets the day before it began. I would travel to attend the convention.

A friend called me that day and told me there was no need to book a hotel; I should just come to Australia. She invited me to stay in her home for five days while attending the entrepreneurial business convention. She said she would pick me up at the airport and pay for my entrance fee to the four-day convention, so I had no need to worry about registration. All was prepared. I only needed to fly to Australia and attend the meeting. God showed me all the signs that I should go, so I said, "Okay, I will travel," and I gave my itinerary, flight number, and time of arrival in Sydney, Australia, to my friend.

I didn't have any time to prepare to travel. I just packed a week's worth of clothes and had one piece of luggage, that's all. By this time, my boys were all grown, so I called them on the way to the airport to tell them I was traveling. I didn't have time to call my bank because I was working the whole day before I left. But I don't need to use my ATM card anyway. I wasn't staying in a hotel, and I had $400 in cash that I withdrew at the Los Angeles airport.

I had confidence in going with the travel plans because I had been invited to attend this business meeting. I was so happy because I had seen the speakers of the convention in a dream and knew I would be hearing them speak. I was so excited. I wanted to see them in person because they were all very successful people, entrepreneurs, authors, and multi-millionaires. I was also happy to fly because I would only be in Australia for one week, then I would come right back to the USA.

When I arrived at the airport in Sydney, no one was there to pick me up. I waited and waited, but my friend didn't come for me. I called, and the phone kept ringing and ringing. Nobody answered, and the convention was starting that night. I was worried, but I prayed to God about what was happening. I didn't give up. I called for a taxi to go from the airport to the convention, but I asked the taxi driver how much it would cost to go to the Sydney Convention Center first.

I went to attend the convention that night, and I brought my luggage with me. After the meeting, I needed to return to the airport to call my friend because I didn't have phone service in Australia. I needed to use the airport's Wi-Fi. There was no Wi-Fi outside the airport, so no one could call me. It was challenging, and it was already 11 p.m. I decided to book a hotel, but I had a problem because my bank blocked my ATM card when I tried to use it because I hadn't called before my flight to Australia.

I used the phone at the airport to call my bank in the USA, but the bank asked me why I didn't tell them that I was going out of the country. I explained that I didn't have the time and now I didn't have money for a hotel. The bank wouldn't approve the charge. My friend didn't call, and I am still waiting to hear back from anyone. I was disappointed again with another trial in my life.

I hoped my friend would call me or answer the phone, but it just kept ringing. So, I sat in the airport with nowhere to go. The Sydney police asked me why I was in the airport, and I explained that I was staying there that night because my friend didn't pick me up and my ATM card was blocked. I showed him my convention tickets and said I needed to stay at the airport. The police officer let me stay, and I took a taxi to the convention the next day and then took one back to the airport that night.

The second day I was still in the airport, the police officer told me he pitied me, and he said to just finish my convention and then fly back. I showed him my plane ticket to show that I would do as he told me. I didn't have a place to shower because I was staying in the airport, so the officer allowed me into a room to shower in the airport. I tried to see about flying back early, but there were no earlier flights, so I had to wait for five days. I was able to continue attending the meeting and stay in the airport, but I was getting no sleep. I was just sitting in the chairs there and made my decision to finish the convention and then return to the USA.

While staying in the airport, I could only drink water, as I didn't have any money for food; it had been spent on the daily taxi rides to and from the convention. I never got discouraged and was excited to meet the speakers at the convention. I knew God was with me and would help me get past my trials. On this last day, I was sitting in the front row at the convention. I met all the people I wanted to see in person, and I got pictures with all of them. I was so happy. My dream came true.

I thanked God for giving me the motivation to never give up. I was full of encouragement from all four days of the meeting. I was so blessed to see these speakers and motivated. I learned from them, and I forgot all about my worries and the situation of staying at the airport. The police had been kind because usually, they only allowed people to stay for more than twenty-four hours in the airport if their flight was changed or delayed for some reason. What an experience I had, with the only thing to give me strength being the promise of God. God answered all my prayers about any of my troubles all the time.

During the lunch break on the last day of the conference, I sat in the corner to charge my phone. I had never felt so hungry, and for five days, I just drank water. A Filipina lady sat down next to me and talked with me. She said that she had met me somewhere, and I agreed, though I didn't tell her that I had seen her in my dream. As we spoke, we realized we had lived in the same place in Cebu, which was funny because I knew her from my dream, not from Cebu. I was happy to meet her.

She asked me where I was staying and if I had family in Sydney. I told her I didn't have any family in Australia and that someone had invited me, but I wasn't staying anywhere because I couldn't get a hold of my friend or use my ATM card. She was shocked. I asked her how she liked the business convention. She said she had only attended today after her friend invited her to come. We chatted and then sat down in the first row together near the speaker after lunch. There were thousands of people at the business convention.

After the meeting, she invited me to go with her to her home. She said, "I'm not driving, but we can take a train. Come to my house and stay for the day before you go back to the USA." I only had one piece of luggage to carry, so I went to her house. We spent the whole night talking, and I never told her that I had met her in my dream.

While I was at her home, she asked how long my visa had been valid. I told her it would be good for one year, but I needed to exit before three months. She invited me to stay and use the extra room in her home, as her daughter was grown, and she could use the companionship. While living with her, I began looking through her library. I started self-studying about health problems and began to write my book, my personal story about my experiences. I said to myself while I stayed at her home, *I will write my story.* She had a business, so I was able to help with the chores around the house while she worked.

While living with the woman, I found the courage to write my life story. I couldn't imagine God putting together all my stories, and sometimes I just didn't understand why all this had happened to me and why tragedies had happened so many times. Over the years, I experienced abuse at the hands of others, and I started to write about each of them, and they are in this book.

To recap, in 1977, I was a victim of brutal abuse by my auntie and almost died when she tied me to a coconut tree and repeatedly hit me with a branch. In 1989, I was beaten by my husband because I ran away from marrying him. In 1994, my foolish/abusive husband tried to choke me to death in a bucket of water. In 1997, I was pregnant and was raped by two men. In 1998, I gave birth on the L.A. highway while the police chased the car. In 2004, my kids were abused, and my Son ended up in a coma. In 2005, I got in an accident and was told I had less than twenty-four hours to live. In 2006, we were homeless for a year because I couldn't work due to my collapsed lung. In 2013, I was in a tsunami. I survived all of these events.

I still believe that God has a plan and a purpose for me to make a difference in other people's lives. My life was full of obstacles and trials but also full of miracles I would never have imagined. Then, I met the people at the convention—entrepreneurs and authors. I stayed in Sydney for three months, then flew to the Philippines, so I was following Australian visa guidelines. They stated that every three months, a visa holder needs to leave the country before returning to Australia. Upon my return, I continued my studies about health products.

A friend of mine whom I met in a church in Melbourne, Australia, while visiting that city, invited me to come to her house because her husband had just passed away. She wanted me to show her how to make my healthy smoothies. So, I went to Melbourne to be with my friend. While there, I taught her about the smoothies, and she liked the health products. I stayed at her house for a few months, and while living at her house, I had a dream to open my business. Knowing I was to start a business, I researched what was required by law and registered my small business in Melbourne, Australia. I named the company Anglicare Miracle Mix, and I started to manufacture my products by myself.

My plan was to sell the fruit/vegetable/herbal mixture in Asian countries only because many poor people in these countries suffer from malnutrition and a poor diet. After all, they cannot afford to buy healthy food. They mainly eat rice, vegetables, fish, and sometimes meat. They need to get enough nutrients or vitamins as they eat sugary foods and drink soda. This plan would fulfill Mr. Grandpa's hope for helping poor people with their nutritional needs, his belief in me that I could have my own business, and the product I created for him.

I could help poor people who experience a lack of nutrition and malnutrition because the Anglicare Miracle Mix is full of nutrients, vitamins, and minerals and is high in antioxidants and protein. It is made from healthy foods, and all the ingredients come from Australia and the USA. My goal was to help the less fortunate people get the proper nutrition. I was motivated to share my health products because I had saved my own life when I was dying after my accident.

When I went back to the Philippines on one of the required three-month visa returns, I demonstrated the products to whoever was in need. I visited schools and gave them smoothies and healthy drinks for the kids, and I saw the Seventh Day Adventist churches to provide them with samples of my product and shared them with the patients in the hospital. I would make the juice and put it in a bottle with my company name on it, and I would give the bottles away to sick patients in the hospital. The healthy juices I created made me happy because the people who suffered from a lack of nutrition, vitamins, and minerals recovered and were becoming healthy. I visited the islands and shared the products. I went on free medical mission trips many times and gave the poor people healthy raw juice with ingredients made from my Miracle Mix products. I am happy to help people, especially those who cannot eat and drink healthy foods.

Chapter 29

Rebuilding the Past

Since I was five years old, my life has been filled with so much drama, trials, and trauma. It was difficult to survive when I faced one problem after another throughout my childhood and into adulthood. Sometimes, I didn't know how I would overcome my pain and forgive those who hurt me when I had been so traumatized. It is tough to forgive others, and it took me a long time to learn to understand wh.? God allowed the incidents of the past to happen, but I grew from them. Reading the Bible taught me to forgive. God helped to change my heart towards my relatives, especially my aunt. Even though she nearly abused me to death, I forgave her. I replaced my anger with love, and I helped her with her medicine and needs for eleven years until she passed away. I got my revenge through forgiveness and love with the help of God.

It's God's grace and mercy that helped me surrender my pain and forgive others. The hatred that was once in my heart was poison to my body. I asked God to help me let go of the bad experiences of my past. It wasn't overnight but over time. It takes time to heal, and what was once tears when I looked in the mirror is now a smile. I helped not only my aunt but all my relatives, especially with Anglicare Miracle Mix, by giving them the product so they would have healthy and nutritious food. I have forgiven them all, and I now have a relationship with my mother.

But it is not only the trauma that I experience, but the trauma my kids experienced because of my actions. My prayer to God is that my boys can forgive me and all my family. I continue to pray, not giving up hope that their pain will be healed once they forgive their Father, their relatives, and me. I know God has forgiven me for my choices, but I long for the day that my sons forgive me. I know forgiving me and others will help set them free.

Forgiveness, as crucial as it was for me to move forward, I felt as if I had no life and I would not find happiness. I raised my kids alone; it was so hard being a mother and Father to the four boys. I was struggling to support them all. When I got sick from my accident, I didn't know how I would have survived without a God in my life. I was waiting for my youngest Son to graduate so I could start building my dream of having my own business. I was so sick and tired of working for someone else, having no life, and making just enough to survive. When my kids managed to support themselves, I was so happy.

In 2017, I decided to push for my dream. I had been a prisoner in my life since I had started working at six years old, yet I was still poor and lived hand-to-mouth only. I went to Australia to begin my new life and business, but I was keeping the recipe that God showed me through reading books to myself. When I began the business and started selling the health supplement to market, I started to put all the pain and scars behind me. This was my new beginning, and my book is to help so many women who are silent about their abuse and to give them courage.

Helping others brings me great joy. Whether I am volunteering or sharing my life experiences with others, I pray that I am making a difference in each person's life. That is my heart's desire – to let others know that they, too, can overcome. With faith in God, being humble and honest as you pray to Him, and forgiving those who caused pain in your life, new things are ahead.

"Break Free from Your Past Positive Affirmations" helps us to think about the importance of the past:

Thinking about the past is necessary for processing our experiences and learning, and this allows us to better shape our future and grow as a person. The problem arises when we can't let go, and we just keep thinking about the same thing over and over again, and we never move forward. It could be a past trauma, abuse, or even something negative that we did or said. These thought patterns become so regular that we can't imagine there ever being a way to break free and leave them behind.

Luckily, the human mind is wonderfully adaptive and capable of change. Use these affirmations to reprogram negative thought patterns and smash through the prison of your past. They will help you come to terms with your experiences, make peace with the past, let go of negative memories, and move forward toward a happier future.

You deselove to be happy, content, and at peace with your past. Get started today with these positive affirmations and take the first step on the path to a happier life.[18]

"You are the master of your destiny. You can influence, direct, and control your environment. You can make your life what you want it to be." -Napoleon Hill

"Before success comes in any man's life, he is sure to meet with much temporary defeat and, perhaps, some failure. When defeat overtakes a man, the easiest and most logical thing to do is to quit. That is exactly what the majority now do. More than five hundred of the most successful men this country has ever known told the author their greatest success came just one step beyond the point at which defeat had overtaken them." -Napoleon Hill

I was born to win. I was born to succeed. I was born to triumph. I was born to conquer all the obstacles and difficulties with the grace of God.

---

[18] "Break Free From Your Past Positive Affirmations," FreeAffirmations.org, accessed April 13, 2021, https://www.freeaffirmations.org/break-free-from-your-past-positive-affirmations/.

Chapter 30
Knockdown Never Knockout

When my life so many times knockout. Since I was a child 5 years old I don't understand why my life was full of trials and obstacles and hardships. I don't understand why God allowed me to suffer a childhood with no parents who cared for me no relatives who cared only my grandparents.

Then I grew up working hard to survive my life full of struggles to work for food and my school needs. When I started growing up the harder my life and the more trials and obstacles I always had difficulty Experiencing.

The road is always dark no light in my path and I kept asking God why I was born suffering.

I cried to God I didn't have anybody to share my story and problems in life who understood me I didn't have a parent to share the hardness of my life and growing abuse and all my relatives ignored me to help me. I cried to God why?

And then I kept dreaming of the United States of America the beautiful place whole America and another part of the World. the beautiful places and scenery shown in my dream. When I Wake up thinking I don't give up.

I remember when I was in elementary I passed that hardship I told myself "I Never Give up".

When I'm in high school it was very difficult and getting harder in my life but I overcame it and told myself again" I Never Give Up."

When I go to college harder and harder in my life I say again "I Never Give Up."

When my family forced me to marry the wrong man because of money and abused me to death. I overcame I told myself "I Never Give Up '

After finishing school, I went to Manila Philippines for another journey to look for a job I kept looking, but I was young and nobody, accepted me. I didn't have a place to sleep, and I was out of money to buy food I prayed to God to help me and I found my second cousin. She has owner small tiny store and she gave her sandals for sale so I could buy food even if I sold the sandals I could not afford to get room to sleep in only to buy food but I didn't have room to sleep." I never Give up."

I pray again that God doesn't leave me in this situation. I keep my faith higher and higher to depend on God's promise the Bible is my GPS. I went to other relatives, but no one helped me, they gave me the advice to go back to the Island of Cebu and work like a housekeeper or planting vegetables. And I ignored it and left. I was hopeless no place to sleep and then.

I Slept the bridges of Quiapo Manila inside the cardboard box I survived for two months and I kept telling and telling myself "I Don't Give Up. "

Until I came to America still nonstop trials in married life and single parents raising my 4 kids alone no end of trials, a nonstop miserable life. But when I read the Bible I keep saying I should not give up I manage to continue to trust God and depending God alone and to survive. I promise myself "I Never Give up "

The Bible gives me comfort peace, Guide like a GPS, and parents and family. when I am reading the Bible and who gives confidence, strength, and peace.

I read the Bible every day and I learned to grow up trusting God alone with unwavering faith. My burning desire is to have peace to overcome these trials make a difference to others and inspire others to Glorify God. These trials of my life can be an inspiration to people who are struggling in life my life story God gave me more faith and to be a blessing to others especially to unfortunate kids.

My dream for this book is to give and donate to unfortunate kids, and education. abused women and abused kids broken families and single parents.

This is my burning desire to make a good example to others to inspire them not to Give up in Life Just trust God with unwavering faith, and" Never Give up".

I learned to trust God even after my life I was knocked down so many times but never, never knocked out, and" Never Gave Up." No matter what I did hardship was only temporary but at the end of the tunnel, there was a light shining in my way.

When I tried to write my book a lot of people discouraged me and my family and friends. No one believes me But "I never Gave Up."

I learned to trust God more and more and I became a stronger person I am not afraid of anything and God is on my side I know God watching me every step of the way.

When I have my life 24 hours to live because of accidents" I never give up "I never quit I never stop praying I keep trusting God I believe in miracles because I know God gives me a lot of miracles in my life.

I am reading others' books and other people's story inspires me their story. and I learn from them.

Now I am Watching my words become action.

Now I am Watching my actions become a habit. I am Watching my habit become a Character.

Now I am Watching my life character become destiny.

Now I am Practicing living with God through prayers daily

Now I am Practicing depending on God's every day with prayer

Now I am Practicing beliefs with unwavering faith in myself and God

Now I am Practicing my faith instead, of doubt and discouragement

Now I am Practicing loving myself and others and humbling myself to avoid negative people and forgiveness

Now I am Practicing myself not doubting myself just smiling, staying happy, joyful, and relaxing

Now I am practicing a (P M A)Positive Mental Attitude.

Prayer is the best way to give your anxieties to God and to exercise demonstrate real faith in Him. Therefore, to eliminate and receive peace, ask God for help, and as the Scripture says, do it with a grateful heart. "Let go and let God" instructs us to let go of the things in our lives that are out of our control. It means not fighting in our physical strength but instead; trusting and with unwavering faith, leaning into God's might. It's the type of surrender that invites God to do the work only a sovereign God can do. And I believe God has a purpose in my life to make a difference in my family others and those who hated me and rejected me. I forgive them all. My dream is to inspire and make a difference to my family and friends and the World .

This text in the Bible inspired me to remove my anxiety and troubles

Psalm 55:22

The Bible quotes discouragement. We are instructed to place our worries onto the Lord so that he may shoulder those burdens for us. There is no need for us to face these struggles alone, especially

Psalm 9:9.

The Lord is a shelter for the oppressed, a refuge in times of trouble.

Psalm 9:10. Those who know your name trust in you, for you, O Lord, do not abandon those who search for you.,

Psalm 34:18 GNT

The LORD is near to those who are discouraged; he saves those who have lost all hope.

The apostle Paul wrote, "We are afflicted in every way, but not crushed; perplexed, but not driven to despair; persecuted, but not forsaken; struck down, but not destroyed"

2 Corinthians 4:8–9). We rejoice that, because of Christ, we are not crushed, despairing, forsaken, or destroyed.

- Psalm 27:1. "The Lord is my light and my salvation—so why should I be afraid? ...
- Proverbs 3:5-6. "Trust in the Lord with all your heart; do not depend on your understanding. ...
- Isaiah 41:10.

Fear thou not; for I am with thee: be not dismayed; for I am thy God: I will strengthen thee; yea, I will help thee; yea, I will uphold thee with the right hand of my righteousness.

Matthew 6:34 –

"Therefore do not worry about tomorrow, for tomorrow will worry about itself. Each day has enough trouble of its own."

Every day, you can offer up your worries to God in prayer. Hand them over to him and tell him to take care of those matters. Do this as many times as needed to surrender to God, and you'll experience God's perfect peace. Stay in the present moment.

Philippians 4:6-7

"Don't worry about anything; instead, pray about everything. Tell God what you need, and thank Him for all He has done. Then you will experience God's peace, which exceeds anything we can understand. His peace will guard your hearts and minds as you live in Christ Jesus."

Matthew 11:28

"Then Jesus said, 'Come to me, all of you who are weary and carry heavy burdens, and I will give you rest.'"

Joseph Murphy

Magic of Faith deals with mental and spiritual laws that promote peace, health, and happiness. The reader will receive a greater understanding of the spiritual laws that govern us and a sound basis for greater faith in the unseen forces for good at our disposal. He teaches "Whatever you do, do it with love and goodwill Pour out love, peace, and goodwill to all. Claim frequently that God's Love and Transcendent Beauty flow through all my thoughts, words, and actions."

Conclusion

I have slowly recovered from all the trauma and put all my pain behind me. I have let go and let God handle everything. I am giving forgiveness to those who caused my suffering, trials, pain, tears, failures, sadness, trauma, troubles, and drama in my life.

I am so thankful to God. He gave me many miracles, such as encouragement faith determination, persistence, strength, and comfort. He taught me how to forgive others.

God saved me and my kids many times in our lives. I cannot thank God enough for His mercy on us.

I am a fighter and survivor of many victimizations in my life. I am a warrior who fights trials. I am free of all the worry and hatred. I forgive myself,

I forget and forgive those who have abused and hurt me. God changed my heart so I could be a loving person who forgives them *all*. My trials become a testimony to others. I am so grateful I give thanks and glory to God for His grace and mercy to my life and my kids.

I'm happy and I want to make a difference in the world. I want to show my life story and share my simple smile with the world. I want to be an example to all people, mothers, women, and kids who are abused.

Never, never, never give up. Never, never, never quit. Keep trusting in God.

Keep believing in your dreams. Keep believing in yourself.

Keep sharing with others.

Keep trusting in your instincts. Keep trusting and loving.

Keep trusting and forgiving.

Keep trusting and stay humble.

Keep trusting and reading the Bible. The Bible is our guide every moment of our lives, like a GPS. Without God, we are lost.

The best is yet to come ahead of us. In this world, we are just passing through. All the things in this world—wealth, education success, fame, and talent—all of it I only temporary.

My kids, I am thankful to God , I am humble and so proud of all my kids. My four boys give me the strength and courage to keep going when I'm so tired and overwhelmed. When I am overwhelmed and loaded with pain and troubles, they smile, hug me, and care for me. They are the only people I have who will assist me. I struggled in my life, and my kids suffered, but they grew into great kids, and they worked so hard in school to help me by taking care of their needs. They are all good honors students, and they have all scholar students from elementary to college and work volunteered with medical missions. They have jobs in schools and communities I am so thankful for my four boys; my sons are my jewels.

My first Son, James, studied at Walawala University, Washington State. My second Son, Joel, graduated from Pacific Union College Angwin Napa California. My third Son, Abraham, graduated from Pacific Union College Angwin Napa, California.

My fourth Son, Joshua, graduated from the University of California and, Irvine.

I am so thankful to God. I give all the glory and honor to our God for His love and protection that He gave to us.

That Inspired Me

2 Corinthians 4:18

"So, we fix our eyes not on what is seen, but on what is unseen, since what is seen is temporary, but what is unseen is eternal."

Romans 8:18

"Present Suffering and Future Glory – I consider that our present sufferings are not worth comparing with the glory that will be revealed in us."

Revelation 21:4

"' He will wipe every tear from their eyes. There will be no more death or mourning or crying or pain, for the old order of things, has passed away."

Matthew 24:35 (KJV)

"Heaven and earth shall pass away, but my words shall not pass away."

About the Author

Born and raised in Cebu, Philippines by relatives, author Jocelyn C. Hughes experienced trauma at an early age, through adolescence, and into adulthood. Despite the mistreatment and setbacks in her life, Ms. Hughes has beat the odds and obtained an education moved to the United States, and started her own business through hard work and perseverance.

In her early adult years, she graduated with a physical therapy certification and moved to Manila, where she worked at a hospital for a short time. Over the years, Jocelyn traveled to other countries and spent time researching the medical and Health benefits of local foods and herbs and studying herbal remedies in each location. Her passion and enthusiasm for healthy eating and alternative medicine started at an early age and was the seed that gave her the inspiration to start her own company, Anglicare Miracle Mix. The company was incorporated in Australia in 2017 and in the United States in 2019.

Ms. Hughes' desire to help others is evident to those who know her. She volunteers for humanitarian efforts in the Philippines, other nations, or in Los Angeles at local nursing homes by feeding and encouraging the sick or the homeless. Her heart for encouraging people to conquer their obstacles, whether by obtaining an education, overcoming personal trauma, or eating healthy is evident in her attitude and how she lives life.

As a single mother, Jocelyn instilled the importance of education as she raised her four boys. All of them were honor students growing up, and each of them had a college education. As a proud mother, she says of her sons, "I am humbled by all of them. God has blessed my boys with the courage to persevere and talent in their careers. I thank and praise God every day for each of them."

My dream for this book is to give and donate to less furniture kids, and education. abused women and abused kids broken families and single parents.

This is "My Burning Desire" to make a difference in the world a good example to others to inspire them not to Give up in Life Just trust God with unwavering faith, and" Never Give up".

My degrees

B S L Bachelors Of Science Eternal Life.

H . U. Heaven University

Angelcare Miracle Mix

Website: www.angelcaremiraclemix.com

Facebook: Angelcare Miracle Mix

YouTube: Angelcare Miracle Mix

Instagram: @angelcaremiraclemix

www.ingramcontent.com/pod-product-compliance
Lightning Source LLC
Chambersburg PA
CBHW041316110526
44591CB00021B/2805